ARTIFICIAL INTELLIGENCE IN HEALTHCARE

A Non-Technical Look At The Future Of Medicine

Constantine Leo Serafim

Artificial Intelligence in Healthcare

For information contact: constantine@serafim.me

ISBN: 9798873761715

Book 1, First Edition: January 2024

DEDICATION

I humbly dedicate my first book to my family and friends who supported me on this project!

But I also dedicated it to all the Unsung Heroes of Healthcare: Relentless researchers, compassionate doctors, caring nurses, and dedicated clinical staff. Your unwavering commitment to health and healing shines as a beacon of hope. Thank you for your tireless efforts, often unnoticed but never forgotten.

With profound gratitude,

Constantine Leo Serafim

"If we are to create processes and policies and build systems that work for the most disadvantaged in our society, then they will work well for the most advantaged."

Constantine Leo Serafim MBCS

Table of Contents

INTRODUCTION

Welcome to my Book. As we delve into the awe-inspiring realm of Artificial Intelligence (AI) and its groundbreaking influence on healthcare, get ready to embark on a journey. I'm excited to tell you about our non-technical book that explores the fantastic potential of AI technology and how it's transforming the healthcare industry.

Join us on this thrilling journey into the future of medicine. I'm excited to share a book that will give you a great understanding of how AI is used in medicine. You'll learn about the technologies, benefits, and challenges of implementing AI in healthcare.

The potential of AI to revolutionise the healthcare industry is enormous. It is exciting to stay up-to-date with the latest developments in this field. Together, let's explore how AI is transforming healthcare for the better.

The book explores AI's recent advances in health and medicine, analysing developments in precision health, clinical decision support systems, and medical data science.

We aim to understand how this exciting technology is shaping healthcare and medicine. You'll learn how it can help improve patient care, reduce healthcare costs, and enhance the overall quality of care. We will also delve into the benefits and challenges of AI in healthcare, including data privacy, ethics, and regulation issues.

Also, we'll look at how AI is shaping the future of healthcare and what it could mean for the industry. By the end of this book, you will better understand AI's role in healthcare and what the future may hold for this exciting field.

Let's get started.

FOREWORD

In a world where technology and healthcare increasingly intersect, the role of artificial intelligence (AI) has become a subject of paramount importance. This book, authored by a computer scientist with an impressive five decades of experience, serves as a guiding light in understanding the profound impact of AI in healthcare for those who may not have a technical background.

The integration of AI in healthcare is not just a story about technological innovation; it's a narrative about how we, as a society, are reshaping how we think about health, wellness, and medical care. In these pages, you will discover how AI is not a distant, incomprehensible concept but a present and accessible tool transforming the healthcare landscape.

The author masterfully demystifies AI, breaking complex ideas into digestible, relatable content. Whether he explains how algorithms assist in diagnosing diseases with greater accuracy or how machine learning can personalise treatment plans, this book makes the science behind these advances understandable and engaging.

Moreover, the author navigates AI's ethical and social implications with clarity and thoughtfulness. Discussions around privacy, data security, and ethical use of AI are conducted in an informative and easy-to-understand manner. The emphasis is placed on the significance of using technology responsibly and ethically.

As a reader, you are embarking on an enlightening journey through the world of AI in healthcare. This book promises to inform and inspire, showing how technology can be a powerful force for good in healthcare when used with care and understanding.

This book showcases the role of AI in healthcare, highlighting how technology is shaping the future of healthcare for better accessibility, personalisation, and compassion.

AI in Healthcare is advancing so rapidly that our conversations about it quickly become outdated. Also, this book is just the beginning of a much larger discussion about how we can use AI to benefit humanity. But don't worry; we hope this book will be a great example of starting this meaningful conversation. We've analysed the strengths and weaknesses of AI, and it's just the beginning of figuring out what we can do to make the most of it. So, let's keep the conversation going.

WHO SHOULD READ THIS BOOK?

This book is an inviting and insightful read for anyone interested in the exciting integration of AI in healthcare. It is specifically tailored for those who have a technical or scientific background. It's ideal for:

General Readers:

If you're curious about how technology changes healthcare but feel daunted by technical jargon, this book is for you. It explains complex concepts in an accessible and engaging way.

Healthcare Consumers:

Patients and family members looking to understand the future of medical care will find this book enlightening.

Healthcare Professionals:

Nurses, therapists, and healthcare administrators who wish to gain a broader understanding of AI in healthcare will find this book invaluable. It offers a clear perspective on the impact of AI on patient care and hospital management.

Educators and Students:

This book is an excellent resource for educators and students in non-technical fields interested in AI's ethical, social, and practical implications in healthcare.

Business Professionals:

This book offers insights into how AI is reshaping the sector for those in the healthcare industry, like pharmaceuticals and healthcare services.

Tech Enthusiasts with Non-Technical Backgrounds:

This book will satisfy your curiosity about how these technologies are applied in real-world healthcare scenarios.

Ethics and Social Observers:

The book delves into the ethical and societal aspects of AI in healthcare, making it relevant for those interested in the broader impact of technology on society.

This book demystifies the world of AI in healthcare, making it accessible, relatable, and engaging for all readers. It invites you to understand the future of healthcare, where technology is not just about machines and data but about enhancing human health and well-being.

CHAPTER 1

WHAT IS ARTIFICIAL INTELLIGENCE?

Artificial Intelligence (AI) is the science of teaching computer systems to think and learn as humans do.

With AI, computers can simulate human intelligence and perform tasks that typically require a human touch. AI can perform tasks that were previously only possible for humans to perform.

These include understanding and recognising human language and speech, solving problems, making decisions, processing visual data, and mimicking human thought processes.

The goal of AI technology is to create machines that exhibit intelligent behaviour.

How does Artificial Intelligence work?

Learning by Example:

Imagine teaching a child to recognise different animals. You show them pictures of cats, dogs, birds, etc., and tell them what each animal is. Gradually, the child learns to identify each animal on their own. AI works similarly. We feed it data (like pictures or text), and it learns patterns from these examples. This process is called "machine learning."

Patterns and Predictions:

Let's say you have an AI that's been shown thousands of photos of cats and dogs. Over time, it starts to notice patterns – like dogs often have longer noses, or cats have sharper ears. When it sees a new photo, it uses these learned patterns to guess whether it's a cat or a dog. It is how AI makes predictions or decisions based on the data it has seen.

Algorithms:

Think of an algorithm as a recipe. Just like a recipe guides you through making a dish, an algorithm guides the AI in processing data and making decisions. These algorithms can be simple or very complex, depending on what the AI is designed to do.

Neural Networks:

This is a bit more advanced, but it's an important concept. Neural networks are a vital part of many AI systems, especially those that deal with large amounts of data like images or language. They are designed to mimic how human brains work, with many interconnected nodes (like brain cells) working together to process information and learn from it.

Training and Improving:

AI systems often start by making many mistakes. However, they learn and improve as they are exposed to more data and different scenarios. This process is called "training." The more diverse and comprehensive the data, the better the AI performs.

Applications:

AI can be used in many areas – from powering voice assistants like Siri or Alexa to helping doctors diagnose diseases, optimising delivery truck routes, and much more.

AI technology is impressive! It can help us create machines that can solve complex problems. Whether automating routine processes or helping us tackle healthcare, finance, or science challenges, AI involves exciting technologies such as machine learning, natural language processing, and computer vision. These technologies help computers learn, understand language, and interpret images.

AI has been a real game-changer, allowing machines to perform tasks that once could be done only by human intelligence. This has opened a world of possibilities for productivity and innovation, which is incredibly exciting!

AI developments positively impact our world, and we're excited to see what the future holds.

Artificial Intelligence, Machine Learning, Deep Learning

Let's break down these concepts in simple terms:

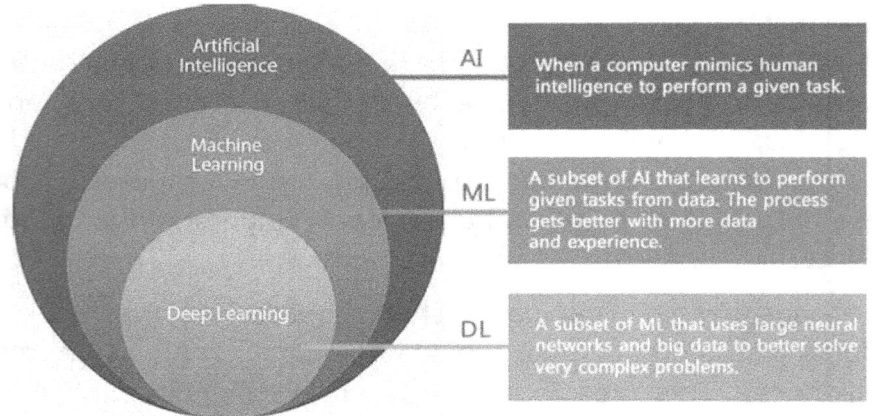

Relationship between artificial intelligence, machine learning and deep learning

1. Artificial Intelligence (AI):

- It's a fancy term for creating computer systems that can do things that usually require human intelligence – like understanding language, recognising pictures, making decisions, and solving problems.

2. Machine Learning (ML):

- Machine learning is a type of artificial intelligence that helps computers learn from data and improve at doing a particular task without needing to be explicitly programmed. Instead of giving the computer specific instructions, you give it data and let it identify patterns and make predictions. It's like giving a specialised tool to the computer, which makes it better at doing certain things.

3. Deep Learning (DL):

- Deep Learning (DL) is like a super-powerful tool within the ML toolbox. Deep learning models are designed to work like our brains, using artificial neural networks with many layers (hence "deep") to learn and understand complex patterns in data. It's perfect for recognising images, processing speech, and understanding language.

So, you can think of it this way:

AI is the big goal of creating intelligent computer systems.

Machine learning is a technique that helps computers learn from data.

Deep learning is a specific method within machine learning that's especially good at handling complex tasks by mimicking how our brains process information through artificial neural networks.

CHAPTER 2

HOW IS ARTIFICIAL INTELLIGENCE USED IN HEALTHCARE?

With the help of advanced machine learning and deep learning technologies, AI is making it possible to diagnose diseases more accurately and personalise treatments based on individual patient needs. By analysing complex medical data, such as patient histories and imaging, AI is helping doctors detect diseases earlier and manage healthcare more effectively.

AI can analyse individual patient data to personalise treatments and improve outcomes. Plus, it helps healthcare providers streamline operations, optimise resource allocation, and automate routine tasks, making everything more efficient.

Understanding AI in Medicine

The healthcare industry is experiencing a thrilling transformation with the help of Artificial Intelligence (AI). AI is revolutionising how we approach healthcare by enhancing the precision and speed of disease diagnosis and treatment plans. Imagine an intelligent assistant for doctors and healthcare professionals who can analyse vast amounts of medical data in the blink of an eye. With AI in medicine, we're empowering doctors to make better decisions and save more lives than ever before.

Potential Benefits of AI in Medicine

Artificial Intelligence (AI) is transforming the field of medical diagnostics by providing an unprecedented level of precision and speed. With the help of AI-assisted diagnostics, healthcare professionals can now identify and understand various medical conditions with greater accuracy and efficiency.

AI-powered diagnostic tools are changing the game when it comes to medical diagnoses. These fantastic tools can analyse vast amounts of medical data in mere seconds, which would be impossible for a human being to do.

This technology allows medical experts to diagnose diseases quickly and accurately, ultimately leading to better patient outcomes. Additionally, these tools can learn and evolve from the data they receive, improving their accuracy and effectiveness. With AI-assisted diagnostics, the future of medical care looks brighter, with more precise and efficient diagnosis and treatment options.

Improved Medical Imaging:

Artificial Intelligence (AI) makes a big difference in healthcare by helping doctors detect abnormalities. AI is especially helpful in diagnostic imaging and pattern recognition. It can help identify even the most minor irregularities in medical data. This leads to more accurate and earlier diagnoses, which is excellent news for patients!

AI is becoming an increasingly valuable tool in healthcare. It can more precisely help healthcare professionals detect conditions like tumours or fractures using various modalities like X-rays, CT scans, and MRIs.

Not only that, but AI can also analyse diverse datasets like medical records and vital signs to identify anomalies and patterns. This technology is helping doctors provide more accurate diagnoses, which can lead to better patient outcomes with early intervention and personalised treatment strategies.

Enhanced Drug Discovery:

Using data analysis, predictive modelling, and other cutting-edge techniques, AI is making drug discovery faster, more cost-effective, and capable of producing innovative treatments for various diseases. With AI's help, we're unlocking new possibilities to improve people's health worldwide.

AI can help streamline clinical trials, automate literature reviews, and even facilitate target identification and virtual screening. It's incredible how much we can accomplish with AI's assistance in creating life-saving drugs. The possibilities for making innovative treatments and cures are endless with AI!

Efficient Administrative Tasks:

Did you know AI can help you focus more on patient care? AI services take care of all the routine administrative tasks, such as scheduling and billing, so medical professionals can focus on what they love - helping people!

More efficient processes mean less paperwork and more time for the things that matter most. So, let AI take care of the boring stuff while doctors focus on making a difference in people's lives.

THE PIONEERING ROLE OF AI IN UNDERSTANDING AUTISM

The application of Artificial Intelligence (AI) in diagnosing Autism Spectrum Disorder (ASD) is a burgeoning field that reflects the broader interest in leveraging technology to enhance healthcare outcomes. ASD is a complex neurodevelopmental disorder characterised by a wide range of symptoms, behaviours, and severity levels, making its diagnosis a challenging and often subjective process. AI's capabilities in handling vast amounts of data and identifying patterns make it a powerful tool in revolutionising how ASD is diagnosed, promising more precision, early detection, and personalised understanding of the disorder.

Behavioural Analysis and Machine Learning are at the forefront of revolutionising Autism Spectrum Disorder (ASD) research and diagnosis. This interdisciplinary approach leverages the precision of machine learning algorithms to analyse and interpret objectively the subtle and complex behaviors characteristic of ASD. Here's a detailed look into how these technologies are being applied:

Researchers utilise video recordings of individuals with ASD to analyse behavioural patterns. Computer vision, a subset of AI, processes these videos to identify nuances in movement, facial expressions, and interaction styles. It includes eye tracking and gaze detection, where algorithms assess social attention by analysing where and how individuals focus their gaze during interactions. Similarly, facial expression analysis through computer vision helps detect emotional responses and social cues, often atypical in ASD.

The advent of wearable technology allows for non-intrusive physiological and behavioural data monitoring. Sensors capture a range of data, from motor movements to heart rate variability, providing continuous, objective measurements that are otherwise difficult to obtain. Machine learning algorithms analyse this data to identify patterns and anomalies indicative of ASD, such as repetitive motor movements or atypical physiological responses to social stimuli.

Language and communication are critical areas affected by ASD. Machine learning is used to analyse speech patterns, including prosody, tone, and rhythm, which might differ significantly in individuals with ASD. Natural language processing, another branch of AI, helps assess language development and use, providing insights into the linguistic and communication challenges of individuals with ASD.

One of the most promising aspects of using machine learning in ASD research is the ability to integrate diverse types of data for a comprehensive understanding of the disorder. By combining insights from video analysis, sensor data, and speech processing, researchers can develop a multidimensional profile of ASD behaviours. This holistic approach not only aids in early and accurate diagnosis but also in tailoring intervention strategies to the individual's unique challenges and strengths.

While integrating Behavioral Analysis and Machine Learning in ASD research offers transformative potential, it also brings challenges, particularly in ensuring data privacy, algorithmic transparency, and ethical use of technology. Furthermore, while these tools provide significant insights, they are meant to complement, not replace, clinical expertise. As research progresses, continued collaboration between technologists, clinicians, individuals with ASD, and their families will be crucial in harnessing the full potential of AI to understand and support those with ASD.

Speech and vocal patterns offer another rich dataset for AI analysis. Children with ASD might exhibit vocalisation, speech development, and language use differences. AI algorithms analyse these speech and language patterns to identify atypicalities. It includes prosody (the rhythm, stress, and intonation of speech), linguistic diversity, and speech development over time. By detecting these subtle auditory biomarkers, AI can contribute to early and more accurate diagnosis, especially in cases where traditional speech therapy assessments might be too subjective or variable.

Neuroimaging data's complexity and high dimensionality make it an ideal candidate for AI analysis. AI, intense learning, is used to analyse images from MRI, CT scans, or EEG recordings to identify neurological patterns associated with ASD. These may include differences in brain structure, connectivity, or function that are too subtle for the naked eye but consistent among individuals with ASD. Similarly, genetic analysis is an area where AI is making significant inroads. Given the vital genetic component of ASD, AI algorithms are analysing genetic data to identify mutations or variations linked to the disorder. It not only aids in understanding the biological underpinnings of ASD but also in predicting it based on genetic risk factors.

Despite the promising advances, employing AI in ASD diagnosis is challenging. The quality and diversity of data are critical in training AI models. Biased or poor-quality data can lead to inaccurate or non-generalisable models. The "black box" nature of many AI models, especially in deep learning, raises concerns about interpretability and transparency, which are vital in clinical settings.

Moreover, integrating AI tools into clinical practice involves technological adaptation, acceptance, and training among healthcare professionals. The tools are meant to augment, not replace, clinical judgment. Ethical considerations, particularly regarding privacy and consent, are paramount, given the sensitive nature of the data involved in ASD diagnosis.

The potential of AI in diagnosing ASD is transformative. It offers objective analysis, early detection, and a deeper disorder understanding. Advancements in this field can potentially enhance diagnostic processes and shed light on the intricacies of ASD itself. However, realising its potential depends on carefully addressing the technical, clinical, and ethical challenges. By working collaboratively, including technologists, clinicians, patients, and ethicists, we can ensure that AI is a beneficial tool to understand and address ASD.

THE INTERSECTION OF AI AND MENTAL HEALTH

Artificial Intelligence (AI) significantly influences mental health, offering innovative approaches to understanding, diagnosing, treating, and managing mental illnesses.

Its application ranges from early detection and personalised therapy to enhancing accessibility and understanding of complex psychiatric conditions. As the prevalence of mental health issues rises globally, AI's role becomes increasingly vital, promising a future where mental healthcare is more effective, precise, and accessible.

Early Detection and Diagnosis

One of the most promising applications of AI in mental health is in the early detection and diagnosis of mental illnesses. Traditional diagnostic methods rely heavily on self-reporting and clinical observations, which can be subjective and often result in a delayed or inaccurate diagnosis.

However, AI can analyse vast amounts of data, including speech patterns, writing styles, and even facial expressions, to detect subtle signs of mental health issues.

For instance, researchers have developed algorithms that can analyse vocal patterns to predict depression or bipolar disorder.

These algorithms look for specific changes in speech, such as monotony, reduced variability in pitch, or slower speech rate, which indicate depressive states. Similarly, text analysis AI can review patterns in social media posts or written communication to detect language indicative of mental distress or suicidal ideation.

PersonalisedPersonalised Treatment

In treatment, AI is instrumental in developing personalised personalised intervention strategies. Mental health is highly individualistic, and what works for one person might not work for another. AI's ability to analyse individual data and predict treatment responses can significantly enhance the personalisation of care plans.

Machine learning models can predict how individuals might respond to certain medications or therapy types based on their genetic makeup, lifestyle, symptom patterns, and previous treatment responses. This predictive capability can reduce the often lengthy and frustrating process of finding the proper medication or therapy, minimising the trial-and-error approach and leading to faster, more effective treatment.

Digital Therapeutics and Continuous Support

AI is also changing how mental health support is delivered through digital therapeutics. These are evidence-based therapeutic interventions driven by high-quality software programs to prevent, manage, or treat a broad spectrum of physical, mental, and behavioural conditions. AI-powered chatbots and virtual agents provide therapeutic interactions to users through their devices, using techniques like cognitive-behavioural therapy (CBT).

These digital tools offer several advantages. They are accessible anytime and anywhere, providing users with immediate, ongoing support. They can be handy for individuals needing access to traditional therapy due to geographic, financial, or social constraints. Additionally, they offer anonymity, which can encourage individuals who might be reluctant to seek help due to the stigma associated with mental health.

Enhancing Research and Understanding

AI significantly contributes to psychiatric research, providing deeper insights into the aetiology and progression of mental illnesses. Through analysing large datasets—such as genetic information, brain imaging, and longitudinal studies—AI can identify patterns and correlations that might be invisible to human researchers. It can lead to a better understanding of the biological, genetic, and environmental factors contributing to mental health conditions and potentially uncover new avenues for treatment and prevention.

Challenges and Ethical Considerations

While the potential of AI in mental health is vast, it comes with significant challenges and ethical considerations. Data privacy and security are major concerns, particularly given the sensitive nature of mental health information. Ensuring the accuracy and reliability of AI predictions is also crucial, as misdiagnosis or inappropriate treatment recommendations can have profound implications.

There's also the risk of over-reliance on AI, which might devalue the human aspect of mental healthcare. The empathy, understanding, and relationship between a patient and therapist are central to the therapeutic process and cannot be fully replicated by AI.

Furthermore, there's the issue of accessibility and equity. While AI can make mental health care more accessible for some, it could also widen the gap for others, particularly those in low-resource settings or those who are not tech-savvy. Ensuring that AI-driven mental health solutions are inclusive and available to all is a significant challenge.

In conclusion, AI's impact on mental health is profound, offering tools for more accurate diagnosis, personalised personalised treatment, and improved accessibility. However, realising its full potential requires careful consideration of the technical, ethical, and practical challenges. By addressing these issues and focusing on a human-centred approach, AI can significantly contribute to a future where mental health care is more effective, efficient, and inclusive, ultimately leading to better mental health outcomes worldwide.

Remote Monitoring and Telehealth

AI in remote monitoring and telehealth amplifies the capabilities of these services, offering advanced analytics, automation, and intelligent decision support.

IoT gadgets can help predict potential health issues. These devices can analyse patient's vital signs and alert healthcare providers to anomalies or deviations from patients' baseline values, allowing for timely interventions. AI assesses patient data to stratify individuals based on risk profiles, enabling healthcare teams to prioritise resources and interventions for those at higher risk. AI helps doctors gain deeper insights into a patient's health status by analysing biometric data like heart rate, ECG, and activity levels. By identifying patterns in this data, AI can detect trends or irregularities that may indicate health issues early on.

Moreover, AI can create personalised patient management plans, considering their health factors and treatment responses. It can even suggest adaptive interventions based on real-time data to help patients manage chronic conditions effectively.

AI-powered NLP can make virtual consultations more natural and interactive. AI can transcribe spoken words into text, making clinical documentation a breeze. Plus, during telehealth consultations, AI can provide real-time decision support to healthcare providers by offering valuable insights and recommendations based on the patient's health data.

AI assists in interpreting diagnostic imaging results, allowing for remote collaboration between radiologists and healthcare teams, and it enhances the quality of remote diagnostic images, improving the accuracy of diagnoses made during virtual consultations.

AI can analyse your communication to understand your emotions and sentiments during telehealth interactions. This can assist in mental health assessments and improve the quality of your care. Additionally, AI chatbots can provide immediate mental health support and guidance. They work alongside human therapists to help you achieve the best possible outcomes.

AI-powered systems can learn and improve over time by constantly analysing data and taking feedback. This contributes to making telehealth services more effective and user-friendly. AI-driven telepresence robots are being used to assist surgeons in remote locations, making it possible to perform surgeries and medical procedures from afar. With the help of AI-based computer vision technologies, surgeons can get real-time guidance during surgical procedures, making them even more precise and safe.

AI in telehealth seamlessly integrates with EHR systems, ensuring that data collected during remote monitoring and telehealth visits is incorporated into a patient's comprehensive medical record.

AI remote monitoring and telehealth applications adhere to regulatory standards, ensuring safety and efficacy. In conclusion, AI in remote monitoring and telehealth brings intelligent capabilities to healthcare delivery, offering personalised, efficient, and secure services. Ongoing advancements in AI technologies and increased adoption by healthcare providers contribute to the continuous evolution of AI-driven remote healthcare solutions.

Predictive Analytics for Disease Prevention

AI predictive analytics is changing the way we approach disease prevention. With advanced algorithms and machine learning to analyse different data types, healthcare professionals can predict an individual's susceptibility to specific diseases. By integrating electronic health records, genomic data, lifestyle information, and wearable device metrics, this holistic approach helps identify health risks before they become a problem.

The best part is that machine learning models discern patterns and correlations within historical data, which means fewer surprises regarding patient's health. These models are tailored for specific diseases like cardiovascular conditions, diabetes, and cancer, making it easier for healthcare professionals to detect and diagnose them early on.

The latest approach to disease prevention is all about personalisation, and AI powers it. What's unique about this approach is that it goes beyond general risk predictions and factors in a patient's genetic profile, lifestyle choices, and environmental influences. Based on this info, it recommends interventions tailored to patients and can help mitigate disease risks.

It's not just about making recommendations; this approach involves continuous monitoring through wearable devices and real-time analytics, which means the patient will get timely alerts and notifications if there's anything they need to be aware of. This allows for proactive management and can prevent health issues from escalating.

But that's not all - this approach helps identify high-risk groups and predicts disease trends for efficient resource allocation and community-level preventive measures. Technology and healthcare are coming together to create a healthier and happier world for all of us!

It's important to consider ethics, privacy, and transparency when maintaining patient trust. With continuous learning mechanisms, AI models can evolve and improve based on feedback and new data, keeping up with the latest medical knowledge.

And when we integrate telehealth with AI predictive analytics, it can have an even more significant impact! This collaboration allows for remote consultations, follow-ups, and monitoring for high-risk individuals, making preventive care more accessible and timely interventions possible.

AI predictive analytics also supports community health initiatives, identifying areas that benefit from targeted education and prevention programs. The technology improves health literacy by providing actionable insights for individuals and communities.

In summary, AI predictive analytics for disease prevention represents a shift in healthcare, offering personalised, proactive strategies to mitigate disease risks. Integrating AI into preventive healthcare practices holds promise for reducing the burden of diseases and enhancing overall well-being on both individual and community levels.

Enhanced Rehabilitation Programs:

Artificial Intelligence (AI) is revolutionising how rehabilitation programs are designed in healthcare. With the help of AI, healthcare professionals can now personalise and adapt treatments for individual patients in groundbreaking ways.

It means more dynamic and patient-specific strategies can be employed instead of traditional, one-size-fits-all approaches to enhance rehabilitation outcomes.

AI technology can design customised rehabilitation programs to fit each patient's unique needs and recovery goals. By analysing medical history, genetic information, physical condition, and daily activity levels, AI algorithms can create personalised rehabilitation plans that ensure patients are neither under-challenged nor overexerted.

This approach optimises recovery and helps patients get back on their feet faster!

Advanced Motion Analysis and Feedback:

Wearable technology is now equipped with AI to help patients during rehabilitation exercises. In real-time, devices like smartwatches, fitness bands, and even intelligent textiles can track patients' movements, force, and form. The AI then interprets this data to provide instant feedback to the patient and the healthcare provider.

Predictive Analytics for Optimised Outcomes:

AI can help healthcare providers predict the recovery path and possible complications based on historical data and predictive modelling.

This fantastic technology allows providers to adjust rehabilitation plans proactively, preventing issues from becoming significant problems and shortening the overall recovery time.

Tele-Rehabilitation and Remote Monitoring:

AI-powered telerehabilitation platforms allow patients to perform guided exercises at home while still being monitored by healthcare professionals.

These platforms use AI to analyse the patient's progress and provide real-time feedback, making rehabilitation more accessible, especially for those with mobility issues or living in remote areas.

Integration with Virtual and Augmented Reality:

AI can help create excellent rehab experiences using Virtual Reality (VR) and Augmented Reality (AR). By turning rehab exercises into games, patients become more motivated to participate and have fun while they get better. These technologies can even simulate real-life challenges and activities to help patients prepare for daily life.

Continuous Learning and Adaptation:

AI can learn and adapt over time. When an AI system collects more information about a patient's progress, it can constantly improve and modify their rehabilitation program to better suit their changing needs and abilities. It means that the patient always gets the best possible Treatment.

Emotional and Psychological Support:

AI can also be a compassionate companion for those going through rehabilitation. With the help of AI-powered chatbots or virtual assistants, patients can get emotional and psychological support, receive reminders to complete their exercises and keep track of their mood and well-being. Additionally, these assistants can even alert healthcare providers if a patient seems at risk of experiencing depression or other mental health issues.

In conclusion, AI is pivotal in transforming rehabilitation programs, making them more personalised, effective, and responsive to individual patient needs. This technological advancement improves physical recovery and enhances rehabilitation patients' overall well-being and quality of life.

Challenges and Considerations in Large-Scale Implementations of AI

Integrating Artificial Intelligence (AI) in healthcare is an exciting opportunity that offers transformative benefits but comes with many challenges. The data quality and integration issues, ethical concerns about the use of patient data, the complexity of AI algorithms, and the evolving regulatory landscape can be overwhelming.

To overcome these challenges, healthcare stakeholders need to prioritise standardised data formats, improve data quality, establish robust privacy frameworks, develop AI models that are easy to interpret, and stay updated with changing regulatory requirements.

A balanced approach emphasising transparency, ethical data practices, and compliance is the key to realising the full potential of AI in healthcare while navigating these multifaceted challenges.

One of AI's most significant challenges in the medical field is ensuring these technologies are seamlessly integrated into daily clinical practice. To achieve this, regulators must approve AI systems, combine EHR systems, and standardise AI products to ensure they function similarly.

Clinicians should be trained on using them, and public or private payer organisations should ensure they are paid for. Finally, these systems should be kept up-to-date with the latest advancements in the field.

As we have seen, one of the most successful applications of AI is medical image analysis. With the help of AI-powered algorithms, doctors can now detect diabetic retinopathy and skin cancer with greater accuracy using retinal fundus and skin cancer images.

It's genuinely unique how technology is advancing to help improve healthcare quality! By using AI to decipher subtle discriminative patterns in pictures, there's much promise that these techniques could also be helpful in other fields of medicine.

It's important to acknowledge that significant obstacles must be overcome before AI can be widely used in healthcare. To make this happen, the focus of AI research must shift towards designing, implementing, and evaluating AI applications that can be used in the real world to improve healthcare delivery.

ML models may be an integral part of AI-powered solutions requiring tweaking. Speaking of healthcare, it's crucial to carefully design and implement these AI systems while considering the evaluation process to ensure they are effective.

Launching AI Systems

Intelligent systems are being developed to improve how doctors diagnose and treat patients. These systems can use collected data to interpret past cases and predict future outcomes, giving patients a head start on treatment. However, doctors may find it challenging to use these systems as they may need help figuring out where to start.

There still needs to be a clear-cut launching point for applying AI in medicine, but as these systems develop, they can significantly improve patient care.

So, when implementing AI-based solutions, the first step is to gather raw materials or data. But, if we want an AI ecosystem that is fair and equal for everyone, we must address information asymmetry and encourage effective collaboration among all the players involved.

Now, let's talk about the pressing needs of healthcare today. We're dealing with a lot of challenges, such as the ageing population, healthcare inequalities, rising costs of drugs and treatments, staff shortages, and various pricing models. It's a lot to handle, severely burdening our healthcare systems.

That's where AI comes in. It has the potential to assist in tackling these issues, but it's also essential to approach it with a discerning eye. We must ensure that everything we're implementing is helpful and appropriate for a healthcare setting. It's a big challenge, but one that's worth tackling!

AI has the potential to revolutionise the way we generate evidence. Some experts even think that AI could replace randomised clinical trials (RCTs), often criticised for being time-consuming and costly.

AI has the potential to revolutionise healthcare by providing faster and more accurate diagnoses for a more significant number of people. With its ability to collect and analyse vast amounts of data, AI is poised to impact the medical field substantially.

AI technology has the potential to make high-quality healthcare accessible to more people. As AI-powered diagnostics become more advanced and accurate, healthcare costs may decrease.

However, it's important to note that even with AI's help, doctors still need their training and experience to ensure precise diagnoses and procedures. Have you ever wondered what would happen if the caring enterprise of healthcare and the research enterprise of AI were to collapse?

Public Awareness

There is still much to learn about how much trust clinicians should have in AI systems when making critical medical decisions. Additionally, figuring out how to design these systems to inspire trust is also something that needs to be explored further.

It's essential to consider various factors, including individual differences, the inherent variability associated with aleatory processes and the rapidly evolving capabilities of AI. And when it comes to applying AI to healthcare, ethical considerations are of utmost importance. It would be interesting to hear different perspectives worldwide and across cultures.

CHAPTER 3

HOW CAN AI IMPROVE HEALTHCARE?

Medical Disease Identification

Do you know what medical disease identification is? It's identifying and diagnosing diseases in patients based on their symptoms, medical history, and other factors. It's important in healthcare because accurate diagnosis is necessary for appropriate treatment and improving patient outcomes. Traditionally, healthcare professionals have done this using clinical knowledge and diagnostic tools like medical imaging and laboratory tests.

Medical disease identification can be a lengthy, expensive, and error-prone process. However, the good news is that with the rapid development of AI technologies, doctors and healthcare professionals are increasingly interested in using AI-based approaches for disease diagnosis.

AI algorithms can analyse vast amounts of medical data to identify patterns and predict disease diagnosis, treatment, and outcomes, which can supplement and improve traditional diagnostic methods.

We can enhance accuracy, efficiency, and patient outcomes by adopting AI-based medical disease identification. Although this field is still in its early stages, we are hopeful that AI has the potential to revolutionise healthcare in the future.

AI-based medical disease identification is making rapid strides and holds immense potential in revolutionising the healthcare industry by making it more efficient and effective. Precise and timely diagnosis is critical for ensuring optimal treatment and enhancing patient outcomes, underscoring the need for reliable disease identification methods.

With the increasing availability of electronic medical records, medical imaging, and genetic data, the demand for more efficient and accurate techniques for disease identification is rapidly rising.

AI technology is revolutionising the healthcare industry by helping doctors identify diseases more accurately and quickly. With the help of machine learning, deep learning, and natural language processing, medical data can be analysed in a systematic and automated manner, allowing doctors to learn from vast amounts of information and identify patterns that may not be visible to the human eye. This technology can address some of the limitations of traditional diagnostic methods.

AI-based medical disease identification is doing wonders in the healthcare industry. It's incredible how these algorithms can be trained using various data sources such as electronic medical records, medical imaging, and genetic data to provide personalised and precise diagnoses and treatment plans for individual patients.

By analysing a patient's medical history, genetic data, and other relevant information, AI-powered algorithms can identify the most effective treatments for that patient, improving treatment outcomes and reducing healthcare costs. AI-powered medical diagnosis and therapy can transform healthcare and significantly improve patient care.

AI-powered medical disease identification has the potential to offer numerous benefits, but it also has certain limitations and challenges to overcome. Machine Learning and Artificial Intelligence in Disease Prediction algorithms must be subjected to careful validation and testing to ensure reliability and accuracy.

Furthermore, data privacy, security, and bias concerns must be addressed to ensure that AI-based medical disease identification is ethical and safe.

Overall, AI-based medical disease identification has the potential to transform healthcare and significantly improve patient outcomes. As technology advances, we must think about how we use it. For example, AI-based medical disease identification has some great benefits!

It can quickly analyse large amounts of data, which can be super helpful when there aren't enough healthcare professionals or when we need access to many medical resources. Plus, it can help doctors make more accurate diagnoses, especially for complex and rare diseases.

By looking at data from many sources, AI algorithms can find patterns and make predictions that humans might miss. AI-powered medical disease identification can do more than improve diagnostic accuracy. It can also help us identify new disease markers and risk factors, better understand how diseases develop, and even inform the development of new treatments.

Moreover, AI technology can monitor disease progression and treatment effectiveness, ultimately leading to better patient outcomes.

By analysing patient data, AI-powered algorithms can help doctors detect early signs of disease recurrence or treatment failure. It can be a game-changer in the healthcare industry! However, it's essential to remember that AI-based medical disease identification has challenges and limitations. For instance, carefully training and validating AI algorithms is crucial to ensure accuracy and reliability.

AI could help with identifying diseases and ultimately improve patient outcomes. However, there are concerns about data privacy, security, and the potential for bias and discrimination in algorithmic decision-making. It's important to carefully evaluate the benefits and risks of these new technologies and ensure they're used responsibly and ethically.

The Use of AI in Medical Imaging

AI technology provides personalised care and improves clinical decision-making, potentially revolutionising our daily lives and society. Medical imaging, including radiology and pathology, is just one area where AI is making a significant impact by improving the accuracy and efficiency of diagnosis. It is impressive to see how AI is changing the game in medicine!

AI in medical imaging is a fascinating field that leverages artificial intelligence to enhance the analysis and interpretation of medical images.

AI algorithms often require standardised image formats. Preprocessing techniques are commonly employed to standardise images for factors like resolution and brightness to maintain data consistency. AI can use advanced filtering techniques to reduce noise in medical images, making structures and details more explicit.

With the help of Lesion Detection, AI algorithms can automatically detect and highlight potential abnormalities or lesions in medical images, which can be helpful in the early detection of medical conditions. CAD systems provide quantitative data and assist radiologists in making more informed diagnoses by offering suggestions based on image analysis. AI can segment medical images to identify and outline specific structures or tumours, providing a detailed map for further analysis.

Deep learning models can segment multiple organs simultaneously, improving efficiency in radiological assessments. AI enables extracting many quantitative features from medical images, providing more information for diagnostic and prognostic purposes. Radiomics involves analysing textural patterns in images, potentially revealing subtle details that may be challenging for the human eye to discern.

AI helps align and fuse information from different imaging modalities, facilitating a comprehensive understanding of a patient's condition. AI ensures that images taken at other times align properly for accurate longitudinal studies or monitoring comparisons.

Generative Adversarial Networks (GANs) can generate synthetic medical images, aiding in data augmentation for training AI models or creating datasets for rare conditions. By generating diverse synthetic images, GANs help improve the robustness of AI models, especially in scenarios with limited real-world data. AI is prevalent in analysing MRI and CT scans to identify tumours, divide them into segments, and plan treatments accordingly. AI assists in detecting fractures, abnormalities, and diseases in X-ray images, improving efficiency and accuracy. AI applications in ultrasound include image segmentation, fetal biometry, and the detection of anomalies.

Natural Language Processing (NLP) extracts information from radiology reports, supporting radiologists in summarising findings and generating structured reports and enables the extraction of valuable insights from a large volume of unstructured radiology text, supporting research efforts.

New models are AI models that explain their decisions, enhancing trust and aiding radiologists in understanding the basis for recommendations. Visualisation techniques, such as heatmaps, help highlight regions of interest and contribute to the interpretability of AI-generated results.

AI-based medical imaging solutions are undergoing regulatory approval processes to ensure that patient privacy and data protection regulations are kept in mind while developing and deploying AI in medical imaging. It's essential to make sure that patients are well-informed and provide their consent for the use of their medical data.

Integration with PACS systems allows seamless incorporation of AI tools into the clinical workflow, ensuring accessibility and usability for healthcare professionals. AI results can be integrated into electronic health records, providing a comprehensive view of patient information for clinicians.

Ensuring representative and unbiased datasets is an ongoing challenge in AI medical imaging. Efforts are being made to address biases and enhance the generalizability of models. Advancements in hardware and algorithms aim to enable real-time processing of medical images, which is particularly important in critical care scenarios.

Collaborations between radiologists, data scientists, and clinicians are crucial for successfully developing, validating, and integrating AI tools in medical imaging.

In summary, AI in medical imaging is a multifaceted field with applications spanning various imaging modalities and clinical scenarios. Ongoing research and collaborations are essential to overcome challenges, refine algorithms, and integrate AI seamlessly into routine clinical practice for improved patient outcomes.

CHAPTER 4

WHAT ARE THE BENEFITS OF AI IN HEALTHCARE?

Personalised Medicine and Treatment

AI-powered personalised healthcare treatment plans are showing great promise. These plans are designed to analyse vast patient data, identify patterns, and customise treatments based on individual characteristics. They can use various patient data sources, including electronic health records (EHRs), genetic information, and lifestyle data.

One of the most exciting things about these plans is that they can help predict disease risk and identify potential health issues before symptoms even appear. That way, doctors can intervene early, and healthcare providers can get a more accurate risk assessment by looking at a patient's unique combination of genetic, environmental, and lifestyle factors.

AI algorithms can even help doctors create customised medication and treatment plans for each patient. They can provide tailored recommendations by analysing individual characteristics like genetics, metabolism, and treatment response. Plus, they can continuously monitor a patient's response to treatment and adjust the therapeutic approach in real-time to get the best results. Isn't that amazing?

AI can analyse genetic information to identify genetic markers associated with specific conditions or drug responses, enabling more targeted treatments. AI algorithms can predict medication reactions using a person's genetic makeup. This predictive ability can help to avoid adverse side effects and increase the effectiveness of drugs.

AI can analyse your lifestyle data and provide personalised recommendations for your diet, exercise routine, and other behavioural interventions. AI-powered devices can remotely monitor your health, giving you real-time feedback based on your health data.

Healthcare professionals can also benefit from AI technology as it provides evidence-based recommendations and treatment guidelines, reduces diagnostic errors, and improves overall decision-making. AI systems can alert healthcare providers when they detect deviations from your personalised treatment plan.

AI technology can facilitate patients' comprehension of their health conditions and treatment plans more conveniently. With interactive interfaces, educational materials, and personalised communication, AI can provide ongoing support and answer questions. Plus, AI-driven virtual assistants can encourage you to stay on track with your treatment plan.

AI has the potential to revolutionise healthcare. However, we must integrate these technologies with caution and careful consideration for ethical, regulatory, and privacy concerns. By working together, healthcare professionals, data scientists, and policymakers can harness the benefits of AI to create personalised treatment plans that prioritise patient well-being and privacy.

Genomic Medicine

Genomic medicine and artificial intelligence (AI) will revolutionise healthcare as we know it. With AI's help, we can harness the power of an individual's genetic makeup to inform personalised and targeted medical interventions.

AI will empower clinicians with unprecedented insights into genetic variants, disease risks, and tailored treatment strategies through sophisticated algorithms and data analysis, fostering a shift towards more precise, effective, and patient-centric healthcare practices.

This synergy between Genomic Medicine and AI holds immense promise in revolutionising how we understand, diagnose, and treat diseases, marking a significant leap towards the era of precision medicine.

AI-powered tools can help us understand our genes better. These tools can detect tiny changes in the genetic code called single nucleotide polymorphisms (SNPs) or other genetic mutations by analysing our genome or specific gene sequences.

This analysis can help us understand how our genes might affect our chances of developing a disease, how it might progress, and how we might respond to treatment. It's incredible how technology can help us take better care of ourselves!

PHARMACOGENOMICS:

Pharmacogenomics explores the influence of an individual's genetic makeup on how they respond to drugs. It encompasses the study of genetic variations that impact drug metabolism, efficacy, and potential adverse reactions.

AI employs sophisticated algorithms to analyse extensive genomic data, identifying specific genetic markers and variations relevant to drug response. Utilising machine learning, AI identifies patterns within genomic information, enabling predictive modelling of how individuals are likely to respond to different medications.

AI in Pharmacogenomics facilitates the customisation of drug treatments based on an individual's unique genetic profile. The precision offered by AI allows for the optimisation of drug dosages, ensuring therapeutic efficacy while minimising the risk of side effects.

AI predicts an individual's response to various drugs, assisting healthcare providers in selecting the most suitable and effective treatment. By aligning medications with a patient's genetic profile, AI improves treatment outcomes and increases efficacy.

AI can help identify specific genetic markers linked to a higher risk of adverse reactions to certain medications. With this valuable information, healthcare professionals can proactively avoid drugs that may cause such side effects, ultimately keeping patients safer and improving their overall care.

AI Pharmacogenomics, at its core, aims to bring a new level of precision and personalisation to drug therapies, leveraging the insights derived from genomic data and the analytical power of AI to optimise treatment outcomes for individual patients.

Clinical Decision Support Systems (CDSS)

"Understanding AI in Clinical Decision Support Systems" is a fascinating read that explores this topic in-depth. It's all about how AI can help medical professionals make sense of complex patient data and provide valuable insights that aid in diagnosis and treatment. From patient histories to real-time monitoring, this technology is changing the game in healthcare.

AI algorithms in Clinical Decision Support Systems (CDSS) are critical in identifying subtle patterns and correlations in patient data. Traditional analysis methods often miss these patterns, but we can find early disease markers with AI, leading to early diagnosis and intervention. That's not all; AI's predictive analytics can also help us forecast disease progression and potential complications, allowing us to manage our healthcare proactively.

AI systems come in handy by analysing patient-specific data, including genetic information, lifestyle factors, and responses to previous therapies. It helps ensure that each patient receives the most effective and appropriate care, potentially improving treatment outcomes.

AI technology in Clinical Decision Support Systems (CDSS) helps provide medical advice and comes in handy for streamlining healthcare operations. By prioritising patient care, managing resources, and minimising the chances of human error, AI helps healthcare professionals provide better patient care while increasing operational efficiency.

By analysing outcomes and feedback, AI systems can refine their recommendations and keep up with the latest medical science and practice. Integrating AI into Clinical Decision Support Systems can offer more accurate, efficient, and personalised medical care.

Clinical Decision Support Systems (CDSS) powered by AI combine various data sources, such as electronic health records (EHRs), laboratory results, and medical literature, to provide real-time recommendations to healthcare providers. These systems are also improved by Natural Language Processing (NLP), which makes it possible to extract meaningful information from clinical notes that were previously difficult to interpret.

Predictive Analytics

Healthcare professionals can now analyse patient data using AI algorithms and machine learning models, making predicting disease progression easier and identifying individuals at higher risk. AI has the potential to revolutionise medical diagnosis and treatment and provide more personalised care and early interventions.

AI insights can incorporate demographic information, lifestyle factors, and biomarkers to generate personalised patient risk profiles. By leveraging these insights, doctors can pave the way for improved health outcomes and a brighter patient future.

Artificial Intelligence (AI), by using vast amounts of data from electronic health records, genomic sequencing, medical imaging, and even wearable technology, AI algorithms are helping medical professionals diagnose, treat, and prevent diseases with unprecedented accuracy. These AI systems use advanced machine learning techniques, including deep learning and neural networks, to identify complex patterns and anomalies in health data that would be impossible for humans or traditional statistical methods to detect.

Healthcare professionals use Artificial Intelligence (AI) to predict diseases early and save lives. Let me explain how it works. First, they collect and process data to ensure accuracy. Then, they train AI models to recognise patterns related to health outcomes. For example, AI can analyse a patient's history, lifestyle choices, and demographic information to predict the likelihood of developing diabetes or cardiovascular diseases. This way, doctors can intervene early and prevent diseases from worsening, saving lives and reducing healthcare costs.

AI technology is helping doctors personalise treatment plans for patients by analysing their unique genetic makeup, environmental factors, and previous treatment responses. It is beneficial in fields like oncology, where AI can predict individual responses to cancer treatments and improve patient survival rates and quality of life.

Hospitals can better manage their resources and prepare for potential needs by predicting patient admission rates and disease outbreaks. It means patients can receive the care they need during critical times without unnecessary delays or setbacks. AI truly has the potential to revolutionise the healthcare industry and help us all stay healthier and happier.

Despite these promising applications, integrating AI in healthcare predictive analysis is challenging. Ethical considerations around patient data privacy, potential biases in AI algorithms, and the need for transparent and explainable AI decisions are significant concerns. Additionally, healthcare professionals require training to interpret and utilise AI predictions effectively.

AI's role in healthcare predictive analysis is undeniably transformative. It's not just about predicting diseases but changing how healthcare is delivered and experienced. AI is at the forefront of a healthcare revolution, from personalising treatment plans to optimising hospital operations and improving diagnostic accuracy. As technology continues to evolve and integrate more deeply into healthcare systems, the potential for improved patient outcomes and more efficient healthcare delivery is vast. However, navigating the ethical, technical, and practical challenges will be crucial for realising the full potential of AI in healthcare predictive analysis.

Natural Language Processing (NLP) for Electronic Health Records (EHR)

Natural Language Processing (NLP) tools can help doctors extract valuable insights from clinical notes, physician narratives, and other free-text information. With the help of these tools, doctors can better understand a patient's medical history, treatment responses, and overall health trajectory.

Natural Language Processing (NLP) makes a huge difference in the healthcare industry by helping us better understand and use Electronic Health Records (EHR). Integrating NLP with EHR systems can improve how we process and interpret health information, leading to better patient outcomes and more efficient operations.

Electronic health records (EHRs) contain a ton of valuable information, like patient histories, lab reports, and imaging data. The only problem is that much of it is in free-text form, which can be challenging to analyse and use effectively.

But that's where natural language processing (NLP) comes in! NLP is an artificial intelligence field that helps computers understand, interpret, and generate human language. With NLP technology, we can convert those free-text notes into structured, actionable data that's much easier to work with.

One of the primary applications of NLP in EHRs is information extraction. NLP algorithms can identify and categorise critical information from clinical notes, such as diagnoses, symptoms, medications, and lab results. This process involves techniques like named entity recognition, relationship extraction, and sentiment analysis.

NLP facilitates better data organisation, searchability, and analysis by transforming unstructured text into structured data. This structured data can be used for various purposes, including clinical decision support, patient monitoring, and population health management.

NLP also plays a crucial role in improving the accuracy and completeness of EHRs. By automatically extracting information from free-text notes and integrating it into patients' records, NLP ensures that critical health information is captured and made easily accessible.

It saves healthcare providers time and enhances the quality of care by providing a more comprehensive view of the patient's health.

Furthermore, NLP enables more sophisticated clinical decision support. By analysing the vast amount of data in EHRs, NLP can provide healthcare providers with real-time, evidence-based recommendations. For example, it can alert physicians to potential drug interactions, suggest alternative treatments based on the latest research, or identify patients at risk for certain conditions. These insights assist healthcare providers in making more informed decisions and delivering personalised care.

Another significant benefit of NLP is its ability to streamline administrative tasks. Healthcare providers spend considerable time documenting care and navigating EHR systems. NLP can automate many tasks, such as transcribing patient interactions or populating fields in EHRs. It reduces the administrative burden on healthcare providers and allows them to spend more time on patient care.

Despite the promising benefits, implementing NLP in EHRs presents several challenges. Ensuring the accuracy and reliability of NLP algorithms is critical, as errors can have profound implications for patient care.

Privacy and security of patient data are also significant concerns, as NLP systems need to comply with healthcare regulations like HIPAA. Additionally, integrating NLP technologies into existing EHR systems can be complex and requires considerable investment in time and resources.

NLP can play a massive role in improving healthcare. It has the potential to convert unstructured text into structured data, provide clinical decision support, and streamline administrative tasks, which can lead to better healthcare outcomes, enhance patient care, and increase operational efficiency.

With the advancement of technology, more healthcare providers are adopting NLP solutions to integrate with EHRs. Integrating NLP with EHRs is expected to become more widespread, further transforming healthcare delivery. However, some technical, regulatory, and implementation challenges still need to be addressed to unlock the potential of NLP in EHRs fully.

Remote Patient Monitoring

There are fantastic AI-powered remote monitoring solutions that can help healthcare providers track patients. These solutions use sensors and connected devices to collect data on vital signs, activity levels, and other health parameters outside traditional healthcare settings. Doing so enables proactive management of chronic conditions and rapid response to emerging health issues.

Treatment Recommendations and Optimisation

AI technology can help doctors provide personalised treatment options by analysing medical data such as clinical trial results, patient records, and medical literature.

By identifying patterns in treatment responses, AI can predict the best interventions and adjust treatments based on individual patient characteristics. This superpower allows doctors to provide the best possible care.

Behavioural Analytics and Lifestyle Interventions

Artificial Intelligence (AI) is doing wonders in the field of healthcare. It's not just limited to making clinical decisions and improving operational efficiencies anymore. AI has now expanded to behavioural analytics and lifestyle interventions, which are crucial for preventing chronic diseases and promoting wellness. By analysing patterns in behaviour, AI can help create personalised, predictive, and preventive health strategies, which is a significant shift from just focusing on treatment.

AI technology can help us understand our behaviours, preferences, and risks by analysing this data using machine learning algorithms, natural language processing, and sensor technologies. By identifying patterns that indicate health risks, AI can help us adopt healthier habits and lead better lives.

By studying data related to our physical activity, eating habits, sleep patterns, and even social and psychological behaviours, we can predict our risk of developing chronic conditions like diabetes or heart disease. Moreover, AI can help identify the early onset of mental health issues by monitoring communication patterns, activity levels, or sleep changes. It's incredible how technology can help us take better care of ourselves.

AI can make lifestyle interventions more effective by personalising recommendations to suit individual needs and preferences. By considering unique behavioural, social, and environmental factors, AI-driven apps can provide customised diet plans, physical activity suggestions, and medication reminders.

They can also offer tailored motivational messages and support, adapting their strategies based on the individual's progress and feedback. It's pretty cool how technology can help us care for our health more personally.

Moreover, AI enables continuous monitoring and support, particularly important for managing chronic diseases and maintaining healthy behaviours over time. Wearable devices and mobile apps equipped with AI can provide real-time feedback and encouragement, helping individuals stay on track with their health goals. They can also alert healthcare providers if a patient's data indicates a potential problem, enabling timely interventions.

Another promising area is the use of AI in cognitive-behavioural therapy and mental health interventions. By analysing speech and language patterns, AI can detect signs of stress, depression, or anxiety. It can also deliver cognitive-behavioural therapy through chatbots or virtual agents, providing accessible and cost-effective support for mental health.

AI can be incredibly useful in understanding our behaviour and providing personalised lifestyle recommendations. However, some challenges must be addressed to ensure everything runs smoothly. One of the biggest concerns is the privacy and security of personal data, especially when it involves sensitive health information.

It's also crucial to ensure that the AI predictions and recommendations are accurate and reliable so we don't receive incorrect or inappropriate advice that could have serious health consequences. Lastly, it's essential to ensure that the personalised interventions are culturally sensitive and accessible to people from diverse backgrounds.

The role of artificial intelligence (AI) in behavioural analytics and lifestyle interventions is a significant advancement in healthcare. It offers the potential to prevent diseases, promote wellness and improve the quality of life. By providing personalised, predictive, and preventive health strategies, AI empowers individuals to take control of their health and supports healthcare providers in delivering more effective care.

However, the full potential of AI in this domain requires overcoming technical, ethical, and practical challenges. As technology continues to evolve and our understanding of health behaviours deepens, AI's impact on behavioural analytics and lifestyle interventions is likely to grow, shaping the future of healthcare towards a more proactive, personalised, and preventive approach.

CHAPTER 5

HOW CAN AI IMPROVE HEALTHCARE?

AI and Drug Discovery

It's incredible how AI is transforming the world of drug discovery and how it can speed up the process of identifying and developing new therapeutic compounds. AI analyses biological data and helps identify potential drug targets for specific diseases.

It allows scientists to understand complex biological networks and interactions, providing insights into the relationships between genes, proteins, and pathways.

With AI algorithms, predicting the potential of large compound libraries becomes more accessible by simulating interactions with target proteins, narrowing down the selection for experimental validation. And that's not all; AI generative models can also design new molecules with desired properties, optimising for factors like efficacy, bioavailability, and safety.

Did you know that AI can help us better understand disease mechanisms and how drugs can be used to combat them? AI provides a comprehensive and holistic approach to disease research by integrating genomics, transcriptomics, and metabolomics. It can even identify biomarkers that indicate how a disease is progressing and how it might respond to specific treatments.

In addition, AI can help chemists predict important drug properties like solubility, toxicity, and whether a drug is a good candidate for further development. AI models can even simulate how drug candidates interact with target proteins, giving scientists valuable insights into how to optimise these compounds.

AI models predict potential adverse effects and toxicity of drug candidates, helping prioritise compounds with a lower risk of side effects and analyse metabolic pathways to predict how the body will metabolise and process a given drug.

AI searches vast amounts of biomedical literature and databases to identify existing drugs that may be repurposed for new therapeutic indications and evaluates the relationships between drugs, diseases, and biological pathways to uncover hidden connections and repurposing opportunities.

In Clinical Trial Optimization, AI analyses patient data to identify subpopulations that may respond differently to a drug, facilitating personalised treatment approaches and assisting in designing more efficient and adaptive clinical trials, reducing costs, and accelerating the drug development timeline.

AI models should be transparent and explainable to build stakeholder trust, especially in critical decision-making processes. Collaboration between pharmaceutical companies, research institutions, and AI startups fosters open innovation, combining expertise to address complex challenges.

Initiatives promoting data and knowledge sharing contribute to a more collaborative and accelerated drug discovery ecosystem.

The availability of high-quality, diverse, and well-curated data remains a challenge for training robust AI models.

AI-driven drug discovery constantly evolves, and we're still figuring out the best ways to validate and approve discoveries. Harmonising AI methodologies with traditional drug discovery approaches is crucial to ensure that AI can be seamlessly incorporated into existing workflows.

In conclusion, AI in drug discovery holds immense potential to transform the pharmaceutical industry by expediting the identification of novel therapeutics, optimising drug development processes, and ultimately improving patient outcomes. Ongoing research, collaboration, and ethical considerations are essential for realising the full benefits of AI in this domain.

Big Data Handling – Drug Research:

Did you know that discovering new drugs requires data, like information about biological pathways, genetic data, clinical trial results, and more? They can process and analyse all this data quickly and efficiently and even extract valuable insights to guide researchers in making informed decisions.

Machine Learning (ML) Algorithms – Drug Discovery:

Machine learning algorithms can help researchers in drug discovery. By analysing existing data, these algorithms can predict how new compounds might behave, making it easier for researchers to decide which ones to test experimentally. It's an exciting way to speed up the drug discovery process!

Biological Targets – Drug Targeting:

AI can help identify potential drug targets. AI can pinpoint molecules or processes that play a vital role in a disease by analysing biological data, like gene expression patterns, protein-protein interactions, and other physical signals. This is important for developing effective drugs. After all, the right target is vital when finding treatments that work.

One of the first steps in drug discovery is identifying and validating the suitable biological targets, such as proteins or genes, implicated in a disease. AI, particularly machine learning and deep learning, is used to analyse biological data and identify potential targets. These algorithms can predict the association between targets and diseases by learning from vast genomic, proteomic, and biomedical data arrays. For instance, AI models can sift through data to find patterns suggesting that a particular protein is involved in a disease process, making it a potential target for a new drug.

Once targets are identified, researchers must find or design compounds that can interact with these targets effectively. Traditional methods involve screening thousands to millions of compounds, a time-consuming and expensive process. AI accelerates this process through predictive modelling. By learning from the structures and activities of known compounds, AI models can predict the properties of new compounds and how they might interact with the target. It speeds up the screening process and helps design new compounds that are more likely to be effective.

Moreover, AI can simulate the drug-target interaction to predict compounds' efficacy and possible side effects, reducing the need for extensive laboratory testing. These predictions help prioritise which compounds should progress in drug development.

AI also facilitates drug repurposing, where existing drugs are used to treat new diseases. This approach can significantly cut down the time and cost of drug development since the drug's safety profile is already known. AI algorithms analyse existing data on drugs and diseases to find matches between approved drugs and new therapeutic uses. This strategy has been particularly highlighted in the rush to find treatments for emerging health crises, such as the COVID-19 pandemic, where AI helped identify existing drugs that might be repurposed to treat the new virus.

Synthesis and Manufacturing:

AI extends its utility to the synthesis and manufacturing of drugs by predicting the most efficient synthesis routes for new compounds. It helps design processes that minimise drug manufacturing steps, waste, and cost. AI systems can also monitor and optimise manufacturing processes in real time, ensuring quality and efficiency.

AI models can come up with new molecular structures. In drug discovery, these models can design brand-new compounds with specific properties. AI can improve existing drug structures by predicting how tweaks might make them work better or have fewer side effects.

AI technology is helping researchers save valuable time and resources in drug discovery. Instead of physically testing thousands of compounds, AI enables virtual screening.

Researchers can use simulations and modelling to predict how drugs interact with target molecules. This helps them to focus on the most promising candidates, ultimately leading to more efficient and effective drug development.

Personalised Medicine

AI can analyse patients' data, including genetic information, to customise treatments based on their unique characteristics. Did you know tailoring medication to a patient's amazing biological makeup can lead to better treatment outcomes and fewer side effects? It's an approach that can make a world of difference for patients.

Artificial intelligence in healthcare has proven highly beneficial, especially in clinical trials. By analysing vast and diverse datasets, including electronic health records, AI can identify suitable candidates for clinical trials. This process significantly speeds up the recruitment process, ensuring that the most appropriate people are chosen to participate in the trial.

As a result, trial participants are more likely to benefit from the treatment, increasing the chances of the trial's success. Using AI in clinical trials is a game-changer and can revolutionise how we develop and test new therapies.

One of the most incredible things it can do is analyse complex and diverse datasets, uncovering novel perspectives that would be unattainable using conventional methods. The possibilities are endless! AI can effectively identify existing drugs that could be repurposed for new uses.

This is particularly valuable because repurposing drugs can save time and resources compared to the lengthy and expensive process of developing entirely new compounds. Researchers can more efficiently explore and develop new disease treatments by leveraging AI to identify potential drug candidates rapidly.

Natural Language Processing (NLP) is a subfield of AI; NLP involves using computer algorithms to analyse, understand, and generate human language.

AI with NLP capabilities has revolutionised the field of drug discovery by enabling researchers to process and analyse vast amounts of scientific literature with ease. With the help of NLP, researchers can quickly scan through scientific papers and identify relevant information, such as chemical compounds, proteins, and biological pathways critical to drug discovery. This saves time and helps researchers stay updated on the latest findings, facilitating the incorporation of new knowledge into ongoing research.

As a result, NLP has become an essential tool for drug discovery; imagine the possibilities of speeding up the process of creating medications and introducing novel therapies to the market. Market faster, empowering researchers to impact countless individuals' lives profoundly.

CHAPTER 6

AI IN HEALTHCARE EMPOWERS PATIENTS

Access to Health Information

Did you know AI-powered tools can help you improve your overall health?

By using virtual assistants, chatbots, and mobile apps, these tools can provide you with relevant health information and personalised insights. You can monitor your health more effectively with biometric data tracking and helpful recommendations. Plus, you can ask questions and receive accurate and timely answers, improving your health literacy.

And that's not all - healthcare providers can also benefit from AI tools by identifying patterns and trends in patient data, allowing them to make better-informed decisions about patient care. Imagine a world where healthcare is more than just a process but an experience that is convenient, accessible, and effective.

AI-powered devices have the potential to revolutionise healthcare delivery and change the lives of patients for the better.

Feeding AI with Information

Teaching an AI is like teaching a child. Just like you would provide a child with information or instructions to help them learn, you need to give an AI with data in a format they can understand.

There are different ways to do this, such as inputting data with datasets, training the AI to learn from the data, fine-tuning it for specific tasks, giving interactive inputs for real-time responses, providing feedback for adaptive learning, updating algorithms for improved functionality, and allowing environmental interaction in the case of AI in robotics or IoT devices.

The best method depends on the AI's purpose, the type of data you have, and the desired results.

Personalised Health Recommendations

With the help of AI, we can unlock the full potential of individual health data, including electronic health records, genetic information, and lifestyle data. By analysing this data, AI systems can uncover unique patterns and correlations, enabling us to receive personalised health recommendations.

From customised exercise plans to dietary advice and lifestyle modifications, AI empowers us to take charge of our health and address specific concerns like never before.

Early Detection and Prevention

Through machine learning algorithms, we have the power to analyse vast amounts of health records and diagnostic information. Recognising subtle patterns can detect potential health issues early on and intervene before they progress. AI technology has the potential to save countless lives and improve the quality of healthcare for all.

Remote Monitoring

We now have the power to constantly check on our health with the help of intelligent wearable devices and mobile apps powered by AI. The real-time data collected by these devices can be easily shared with healthcare providers, which enables remote monitoring and immediate intervention if any irregularities or health issues are detected.

This groundbreaking technology is especially beneficial for individuals with chronic illnesses as it empowers them to take charge of their health and well-being like never before.

Medication Management

Did you know that taking medication on time and in the correct dosage is essential for your health? Well, AI-powered solutions are here to help! By sending personalised reminders through mobile apps or messaging platforms, AI can ensure you never forget to take your medication.

AI can analyse the data to provide insights about how well you're sticking to your medication routine. This can help your healthcare provider make better decisions about your care. With AI-powered medication adherence solutions, you'll get all the support you need to take charge of your health!

Behavioural Support

By utilising AI-powered health apps and chatbots, individuals can receive personalised advice and support for behaviour change, empowering them to make positive and lasting changes.

By considering an individual's unique preferences, habits, and goals, AI can provide tailored recommendations for healthier living, enabling individuals to achieve their full potential and live their best lives.

Empowering Patient-Doctor Communication

Did you know AI can help make patient health information accessible to patients and healthcare providers? This can lead to a more informed and empowered patient population, which can help facilitate productive conversations between patients and providers and create a more collaborative approach to healthcare.

Overall, the integration of AI in healthcare empowers patients by providing them with information, personalised insights, and support. AI is transforming the healthcare experience into a more proactive, individualised, collaborative endeavour between patients and their providers.

Wearable Devices and Health Applications

Did you know that AI-powered wearable devices and health applications can make a difference in promoting a healthier lifestyle?

By using artificial intelligence to monitor, analyse, and provide personalised insights, these technologies help you take control of your well-being. Here are just a few ways they can contribute to a happier, healthier you.

Activity Tracking and Fitness Monitoring

Did you know that wearables with accelerometers and gyroscopes can help you keep track of your movement patterns? They can provide information on your steps, the distance you've covered, and how long you've been active. Some devices even have GPS tracking, which can map your outdoor activities and give you more accurate distance measurements.

Did you know that machine learning algorithms can help you achieve your fitness goals? By analysing your past activity data, these algorithms can identify patterns and trends and provide tailored recommendations to help you stay on track.

Moreover, they are adaptive and can adjust their advice based on your progress and changes in your activity patterns over time. So, let's get moving and achieve your fitness dreams together!

Health Monitoring

Did you know that wearables with optical sensors can monitor your heart rate continuously, giving you insights into your resting heart rate, exercise-related heart rate, and recovery rates?

And suppose you're looking for a non-invasive way to track your blood pressure regularly. In that case, blood pressure monitors are now available, which makes it super easy to do so.

Hey there! Did you know AI algorithms can analyse vital signs and detect deviations from standard patterns? It's impressive how wearables can alert you and your healthcare provider to any abnormalities, prompting further investigation.

Personalised Recommendations

AI technology is impressive at analysing your fitness behaviour, including your preferred exercise types, activity levels, and responses to different training intensities. Based on this analysis, we can create personalised workout plans and nutritional recommendations for you!

Did you know that getting real-time feedback during your workouts can help you maintain proper form, adjust exercise intensity, and optimise your training sessions? Our adaptive coaching considers changes in your fitness levels, health conditions, and personal goals to help you achieve the best results possible.

Chronic Disease Management

Did you know that there are wearables that can help individuals with diabetes by continuously monitoring their glucose levels? That's right! These devices can provide valuable insights into blood sugar levels throughout the day. Additionally, continuous heart rate monitoring can also be beneficial in managing cardiovascular conditions.

Maintaining medication schedules is essential to ensure you get the most out of your treatment. Fortunately, there are some tremendous.

AI-powered apps out there that can help you stay on track with your medication schedule. These apps can send you timely reminders and adjust your schedule based on your feedback and prescription changes. These apps let you control your health and achieve better outcomes.

Stress and Mental Health

Did you know that wearable devices with fancy sensors can help you keep an eye on your stress levels? Cool, right? These devices can measure your heart rate variability and skin conductance, two crucial stress indicators in your body.

Not only that, but they can also track your sleep quality and activity levels, giving you a complete picture of your stress. By keeping track of all your activities and monitoring your stress levels, wearable devices can assist you in managing stress effectively and enhancing your overall health and well-being.

It is worth noting that the use of AI-powered virtual assistants and chatbots is rising in the mental health field. AI tools are proving to be highly beneficial in providing support to individuals who are struggling with mental health issues. From offering effective coping strategies to suggesting mindfulness exercises, these chatbots can help people manage their symptoms and enhance their mental well-being.

One of the most remarkable features of these chatbots is mood tracking. This allows you to monitor your mood levels every day. Did you know that chatbots can help you track your mood and identify patterns related to your mental health? This is especially helpful for people who might be dealing with mood disorders, depression, or anxiety.

By keeping track of your mood, you can better understand your emotions and find ways to manage your symptoms more effectively. I hope this information helps! Did you know that AI-powered chatbots and virtual assistants can transform how mental health is addressed?

They can provide practical and easily accessible support to people who need it the most. It's incredible how technology can help make mental health care more approachable and friendly.

Health Data Integration

Imagine a world where you can wear a device that effortlessly syncs with your electronic health records, giving your healthcare provider access to accurate and up-to-date patient information during appointments.

The potential for improving patient outcomes and transforming healthcare is limitless. Moreover, wearables provide a comprehensive and holistic view of your health when combined with other health apps and devices, such as smart scales and blood glucose monitors.

By analysing your health data, AI generates valuable insights to help you and healthcare professionals make informed decisions about your health. This way, you can easily understand the relationships between different health metrics and take the necessary steps to improve your overall well-being.

Preventive Healthcare

Did you know that machine learning models can predict health risks based on lifestyle factors, genetic information, and historical health data? And the best part is that you can receive personalised recommendations to help you mitigate any identified risks. These recommendations may include simple changes in your diet or exercise habits.

Did you know that wearable devices with electrocardiogram (ECG) monitoring can help you keep track of your heart's health? These devices can detect abnormal heart rhythms, such as atrial fibrillation, which can be an early warning for possible cardiovascular health issues.

With this innovative approach to heart health monitoring, you can get a detailed analysis of your heart's electrical activity and stay ahead of potential health problems. It's always better to take the necessary precautions and stay healthy!

Community and Social Engagement

You can join in on challenges and compete with your friends or community members using AI-driven features. Leaderboards and achievements motivate you and keep you engaged for the long haul.

Did you know that AI-powered algorithms can help you find like-minded individuals with similar health goals? These algorithms analyse your health history and fitness levels to create personalised virtual support groups. You can join a community of people who share your health goals.

You can participate in group challenges, exchange tips and advice, and share your progress and victories. Joining this community will allow you to connect with others, share your experiences, and inspire each other. With the help of AI-powered virtual support networks, you'll never feel alone on your journey towards a healthier lifestyle.

With the ability to provide real-time monitoring, adaptive recommendations, and social engagement, using AI in these devices allows for a highly personalised and comprehensive approach to promoting a healthier lifestyle. Wearable devices and similar technologies collect data that can be analysed and used to provide customised recommendations, making it easier for individuals to maintain a healthy lifestyle.

The rapid advancement of these technologies is about to revolutionise preventive healthcare and personalised wellness. Brace yourself for a proactive and efficient approach to healthcare management as never seen before.

I'm excited to see how integrating AI in wearable devices and health applications will revolutionise the healthcare industry and change how we perceive healthcare and wellness.

CHAPTER 7

BENEFITS AND CHALLENGES OF AI IN HEALTHCARE

Integrating Artificial Intelligence (AI) into healthcare is more complex. Various challenges must be addressed, such as ensuring data privacy, maintaining quality, and considering ethical and legal considerations, biases, and regulatory compliance. One of the primary concerns is keeping sensitive patient data confidential and secure against potential breaches, as AI systems require access to large volumes of such data.

Also, the effectiveness of AI in healthcare heavily relies on the quality and availability of data, and issues such as inaccuracies, gaps, and lack of standardisation can impede AI performance.

Using AI in healthcare, there are some important ethical and legal considerations that we need to keep in mind. For example, we want to make sure that patients are fully aware of how their data is being used and that the decisions made by AI systems are transparent and fair. We also need to be accountable for any mistakes or misdiagnoses that might occur along the way.

Another challenge with AI systems is ensuring they don't reinforce biases in the data they learn from. We want to ensure everyone is treated equally, regardless of origin or background. That's why it's essential to take the time to consider these issues and develop strategies to address them carefully.

Finally, one of the biggest challenges in healthcare is understanding and following all the different rules and regulations. When using AI in healthcare, it's essential to follow strict guidelines to ensure patients are well taken care of and their data is kept safe.

These rules can differ depending on where you are and can change as technology evolves. It's up to healthcare providers and developers to work together to ensure AI systems meet all the requirements and provide excellent patient care.

Improving Patient Outcomes

Artificial Intelligence is transforming the healthcare industry. AI-powered technologies lead to early disease detection, personalised treatment plans, and enhanced medical imaging analysis. AI in healthcare is helping doctors make more informed decisions by continuously monitoring patient vitals and detecting subtle changes that might go unnoticed by human clinicians.

This proactive approach enables early intervention and prevents adverse events, ultimately improving patient outcomes. Moreover, AI algorithms can assist healthcare providers in developing tailored treatment plans based on individual patient characteristics, such as genetic makeup, lifestyle, and medical history. This precision medicine approach ensures patients receive the most effective and personalised care, improving outcomes and reducing side effects.

AI also plays a crucial role in early disease detection. With its ability to process vast amounts of data within seconds, AI can quickly analyse patient records, genetic information, and imaging results. AI empowers healthcare professionals to detect possible indications of diseases in their early stages before any symptoms manifest themselves.

Understanding these advancements can help us appreciate the potential of AI to transform the future of medicine, making it more efficient, accurate, and patient-centric. It's about more than just the early detection of diseases but also preventing them altogether. AI can identify patterns and trends in healthcare data that may need to be easily discernible through human analysis. This is achieved through the analysis of vast amounts of data. This valuable insight helps healthcare providers develop personalised prevention strategies for individuals and communities.

For example, AI can help identify populations at high risk for infectious diseases and assist in developing vaccination campaigns or public health initiatives. AI revolutionises healthcare by helping professionals detect diseases at their earliest stages and implement targeted preventive interventions.

With AI, healthcare providers can create personalised treatment plans tailored to individual patients, improving outcomes and better patient experiences.

By leveraging AI technology, we can transform healthcare into a proactive system that focuses on maintaining health and preventing diseases before they become life-threatening.

AI technology continues to make considerable strides in the healthcare industry, offering the immense potential to enhance efficiency and reduce costs. However, we must acknowledge the challenges of implementing AI in precision treatment planning. Privacy and security concerns, ethical considerations, and the need for human oversight are all critical factors to address.

Additionally, AI systems must be continuously validated and updated to ensure accuracy and reliability. Despite the challenges, the future of precision treatment planning looks promising with the integration of AI into healthcare practices. Healthcare providers can make more informed decisions by leveraging AI algorithms, resulting in better patient outcomes.

One significant area where AI can drive efficiency is the automation of administrative tasks. Hospitals and healthcare facilities are often burdened with time-consuming paperwork, data entry, and appointment scheduling. AI-powered systems can automate regular tasks, freeing doctors' valuable time to concentrate on more vital aspects of patient care. Not only does this reduce the administrative burden, but it also minimises the chances of manual errors and improves overall efficiency.

Can AI help healthcare organisations optimise resources and reduce costs? By analysing patient data, AI algorithms can predict patient flow, bed occupancy rates, and demand for healthcare services, allowing hospitals to allocate resources efficiently and reduce wait times. AI can also help manage inventory, ensure that medical supplies and medications are stocked adequately, minimise waste, and control costs.

Healthcare organisations consider cost reduction critical, and artificial intelligence can effectively contribute to achieving this goal. Automating routine tasks and enhancing operational efficiency enable healthcare organisations to conserve precious resources and channel them towards better patient care. AI-powered systems can also help identify areas of inefficiency and suggest process improvements, leading to cost savings in the long run.

In conclusion, integrating AI in healthcare can revolutionise healthcare delivery, from automating administrative tasks to improving diagnostic accuracy and resource allocation. Embracing AI technology can lead to improved patient outcomes, reduced administrative burden, and cost savings, ultimately transforming the future of medicine.

With AI, healthcare professionals can focus on providing quality patient care. At the same time, AI algorithms handle administrative tasks, making healthcare operations more efficient. While AI implementation in healthcare offers numerous benefits, addressing data privacy is essential. As AI relies heavily on data, protecting patient information is crucial. Enforcing strong security measures to safeguard sensitive data from unauthorised access and breaches is vital.

In conclusion, the integration of AI in healthcare has the potential to streamline administrative tasks and enhance efficiency in various aspects of healthcare operations. By automating processes, optimising data management, and improving supply chain logistics, AI enables healthcare professionals to focus more on providing quality patient care.

As AI continues to evolve, non-technical individuals interested in AI in healthcare need to understand its potential and stay abreast of the latest developments in this exciting field.

Automating Repetitive Processes with AI

In the rapidly evolving world of healthcare, artificial intelligence (AI) is revolutionising how we approach various medical tasks and processes. One area where AI has made significant strides is automating repetitive processes, streamlining operations, and improving overall efficiency in healthcare.

Repetitive tasks are integral to healthcare but can often be time-consuming, prone to errors, and drain resources. AI technology offers a solution by automating these mundane and repetitive processes, allowing doctors to focus on more critical aspects of patient care.

One of the significant advantages of utilising AI for automating repetitive processes is its enhanced accuracy. AI algorithms can quickly analyse vast amounts of data with incredible precision, minimising the potential for human error.

This accuracy is particularly valuable in medical data entry, where even a tiny mistake can have significant consequences. By automating this process, AI reduces the chances of errors and ensures the integrity of patient records.

AI-powered automation also significantly speeds up processes traditionally taking hours or even days to complete. For instance, AI algorithms can quickly analyse medical images, such as X-rays or MRI scans, identifying abnormalities and assisting radiologists in making accurate diagnoses. This saves time and allows physicians to provide timely treatment options, ultimately improving patient outcomes.

Furthermore, automating repetitive processes with AI enables healthcare organisations to optimise resource allocation. By delegating time-consuming tasks to AI systems, healthcare professionals can focus on more complex and critical aspects of their work. This results in improved productivity, reduced burnout, and better utilisation of valuable human resources.

It is crucial to note that AI does not replace healthcare professionals but complements their expertise. AI is a powerful tool, augmenting their skills and aiding decision-making processes. Ethical considerations, privacy concerns, and ensuring the transparency of AI algorithms are essential factors that must be carefully managed to maintain trust in the healthcare system.

In conclusion, automating repetitive processes with AI can revolutionise healthcare by improving accuracy, speeding up processes, and optimising resource allocation. As AI advances, healthcare professionals and policymakers must embrace its potential and collaborate to ensure a future where AI enhances patient care and transforms the healthcare industry.

Ethics and Privacy Concerns

As the field of Artificial Intelligence (AI) in healthcare continues to advance rapidly, it is crucial to address privacy concerns that arise alongside these technological advancements. While AI has the potential to revolutionise the healthcare industry, it also brings forth a myriad of ethical dilemmas that must be carefully navigated.

Bias is a significant concern in AI for healthcare. Machine learning algorithms can only be as unbiased as the data they rely on. It is essential to ensure that the data used to train these algorithms is free from bias. Suppose the training data used to develop AI models needs to be revised. In that case, it can lead to discriminatory outcomes that disproportionately affect certain groups of patients.

For instance, if the AI system is trained on historical medical data that is biased against certain racial or ethnic groups, it may perpetuate these biases and contribute to healthcare disparities. Therefore, ensuring that AI systems are developed using diverse and representative datasets is crucial to avoid perpetuating inequality and bias in healthcare.

Another critical ethical consideration is the issue of patient privacy. As AI systems analyse and process vast amounts of personal health data, the potential for unauthorised access, misuse, or data breaches becomes a significant concern. Strict privacy protocols and robust security measures must be in place to safeguard patient information.

This includes using encryption techniques, anonymising data, and obtaining informed consent from patients to use their data for AI research and analysis. Additionally, healthcare organisations must adhere to stringent General Data Protection Regulation to ensure compliance and protect patients' privacy rights.

Furthermore, transparency and Explainability are vital aspects when implementing AI in healthcare. Healthcare providers must understand how AI algorithms make decisions and recommendations. Developing AI systems that provide clear explanations and justifications for their choices can help build confidence and ensure that healthcare professionals can confidently rely on AI-driven insights.

Lastly, the potential impact of AI on healthcare professionals and the workforce must also be considered. While AI has the potential to augment clinical decision-making and streamline administrative tasks, it may also raise concerns about job displacement and the devaluation of human expertise. It is vital to balance AI's capabilities and healthcare professionals' skills, ensuring that AI enhances, rather than replaces, human capabilities.

In conclusion, integrating AI into healthcare brings great promise for improving patient outcomes and revolutionising medical practice. However, it is crucial to address the ethical considerations and privacy concerns that arise to ensure that AI is developed and implemented fairly and transparently and respects patient privacy.

By proactively addressing these issues, we can harness the true potential of AI in healthcare while upholding the highest ethical standards and preserving patient trust.

Data Privacy and Security in AI-Driven Healthcare

As Artificial Intelligence (AI) continues to revolutionise the healthcare industry, it is crucial to address data privacy and security concerns.

In AI-powered healthcare systems, vast amounts of patient data are collected and analysed for personalised and accurate medical insights.

This data includes sensitive information such as medical history, diagnoses, and genetic data, making it imperative to safeguard it from unauthorised access or misuse. Stringent privacy regulations and protocols have been established to protect patient privacy.

Compliance with these regulations ensures that healthcare organisations handle patient information responsibly and securely. Privacy and security must be a top priority when using AI algorithms in healthcare. This means protecting patient data through encryption and anonymisation while allowing AI algorithms to gain valuable insights. Cybersecurity protocols must be robust to prevent data breaches and unauthorised access to sensitive information.

Collaboration between AI developers, healthcare providers, and cybersecurity experts is essential to avoid potential vulnerabilities. Patients should be informed about how their data will be used and should have control over it. By prioritising data protection, we can unleash the full potential of AI in transforming healthcare while safeguarding patient privacy.

Ensuring Fairness and Bias Mitigation in AI Algorithms

AI algorithms are excellent tools that are revolutionising the healthcare industry. They can improve patient outcomes, increase efficiency, and reduce costs. However, as we integrate AI into our healthcare systems, addressing fairness and bias mitigation in these algorithms is essential. AI algorithms are designed to learn from vast amounts of data, which helps them make predictions and decisions.

However, if the data used to train these algorithms is biased, it can lead to unfair or discriminatory outcomes. For example, suppose an AI algorithm is trained on patient data predominantly from one demographic group. In that case, it may need help recognising other demographic groups' unique characteristics and risks.

We must take a holistic approach to ensure fairness and bias mitigation in AI algorithms. Firstly, we should collect data representing the diverse populations healthcare systems serve. This means collecting data from various demographic groups, including those historically underrepresented in healthcare research. By incorporating a wide range of data, algorithms can be trained to recognise and account for different populations' unique needs and risks.

Secondly, transparency and Explainability of AI algorithms are essential. Healthcare professionals and patients must understand how these algorithms make predictions or decisions. By providing explanations and insights into the underlying process, individuals can better assess the fairness and accuracy of AI-generated recommendations. This transparency can also help identify and rectify any biases that may be present in the algorithms.

Furthermore, regular audits and evaluations of AI algorithms are necessary to ensure fairness and mitigate bias. These audits can identify potential biases and disparities over time as the algorithms interact with real-world data. By periodically reviewing and refining the algorithms, healthcare organisations can improve their performance and minimise any unintended consequences.

Lastly, a collaboration between technical experts and healthcare professionals is vital. In developing and deploying AI algorithms, involving diverse stakeholders, including those representing different specialities, patient advocacy groups, and ethicists, is essential. Their insights and perspectives can help identify potential biases, ensure fairness, and address ethical concerns.

In conclusion, AI can potentially transform healthcare. Still, we must address fairness and bias mitigation in AI algorithms. By collecting representative data, providing transparency, conducting regular audits, and fostering collaboration, healthcare organisations can harness the full potential of AI while ensuring fair and unbiased outcomes for all patients.

CHAPTER 8

ON-GOING TRENDS AND RISKS IN AI AND MEDICINE

It's fascinating to see how the healthcare industry is evolving with the help of AI technology and tools. Factors like the global pandemic, ageing populations, and rising healthcare costs have significantly shaped the industry and created new opportunities for AI to add value.

As per many survey results, data annotation is emerging as a fundamental AI technology, and text has now become the most used data type in AI applications, paving the way for new possibilities and inspiring innovations in the field. Clinical decision-making and disease diagnosis are critical areas of medicine where AI is making an impact. Surveys also show clinical notes and improve documentation.

Clinical Decision Support

Incorporating Artificial Intelligence (AI) in Clinical Decision Support (CDS) systems can significantly improve healthcare. It helps healthcare providers make informed, data-driven, and patient-specific decisions.

With AI in CDS, we can analyse and interpret vast and complex healthcare data, including electronic health records, medical imaging, laboratory results, and genetic information. It allows for synthesising comprehensive patient insights, enabling personalised treatment plans, and improving diagnostic accuracy. It's incredible how technology can help us enhance healthcare quality.

It's interesting to note that AI-powered tools can assist doctors in detecting diseases at an early stage. These tools can analyse data and identify patterns that humans may overlook. It helps predict a patient's progress and suggests the most effective treatment options.

For example, in medical imaging, AI algorithms can quickly and accurately find that a person has cancer. It's incredible how technology can help us take better care of ourselves!

AI systems can be beneficial in healthcare. They can stay up-to-date with the latest medical research and guidelines, instrumental in managing complex or rare conditions. Not only that, but AI can also help assess and manage risks by analysing patient data and predicting potential complications.

AI improves healthcare by providing accurate, efficient, and personalised patient care. However, it's essential to remember that integrating AI into clinical decision-making requires us to be mindful of ethical, privacy, and security issues.

We must ensure that patient data is handled responsibly and that AI systems are transparent and unbiased. It's also essential for healthcare providers to maintain their critical decision-making role while using AI to assist them rather than replace human judgment.

Overall, AI in clinical decision support improves healthcare, allowing us to continuously adapt to new medical insights and patient data.

Pharmacovigilance

Have you ever heard of Pharmacovigilance? It's an extraordinary field of science that helps us detect, assess, understand, and prevent any adverse effects or other drug-related problems. Are you curious to know more about it? Let's dive in and explore together! It's essential work!

Pharmacovigilance is all about keeping track of the safety of medicines. It's a scientific and systematic way of detecting, assessing, understanding, and preventing any adverse drug reactions (ADRs) and other drug-related problems that might occur. It is essential to ensure that any medication out there is safe for everyone to use, from when it's first developed in clinical trials to when it's widely available to the public.

Let me tell you a little about how we keep track of drug safety. We collect and analyse data from various sources, like healthcare professionals, patients, and regulatory agencies. We use electronic healthcare records and scientific literature to identify potential issues. Once we have the data, we carefully analyse it to determine if any health problems are related to the medication or just coincidence.

It involves assessing the risks and benefits of drugs and ensuring only those with favourable profiles are approved and remain on the market. This assessment is ongoing as new evidence can emerge anytime throughout a drug's life on the market.

If any risks are identified, pharmacovigilance activities may lead to changes in how medicine is used, updates to patient information leaflets, additional warnings on labels, or, in some cases, withdrawal of the drug from the market.

Pharmacovigilance is all about keeping patients safe and healthy! It's a team effort involving healthcare professionals, patients, and drug manufacturers, all working together to ensure that medicines are as safe as possible. Regulatory authorities oversee everything to ensure we're all on the same page. Pharmacovigilance aims to give everyone the information they need to make informed decisions about medicines so patients get the best care possible!

Incorporating Artificial Intelligence (AI) into pharmacovigilance can help us monitor and ensure drug safety more effectively. AI has unique data processing and pattern recognition capabilities that can significantly improve our ability to detect, assess, understand, and prevent adverse drug reactions (ADRs) and other drug-related problems. Thinking about how AI can help us improve healthcare and keep people safe is exciting.

Imagine a world where medical researchers can quickly access comprehensive data from various sources like electronic health records, pharmaceutical databases, and patient reports.

Thanks to the power of AI, this dream is now a reality! With machine learning algorithms, AI can identify patterns and correlations in large datasets that traditional methods might miss.

This breakthrough technology has the potential to revolutionise how we approach healthcare research and improve the efficiency of data collection. Let's embrace the exciting new possibilities that AI has to offer!

It's essential to catch possible side effects of medications as soon as possible, especially the rare or unexpected ones. That's where AI can help! Analysing complex data can predict potential adverse effects of drugs and help regulators decide how to label, use, or withdraw them from the market. It helps speed up decision-making and ensures everyone stays safe and healthy.

AI tools can be incredibly helpful in monitoring drug safety. They can provide real-time insights into how medicines affect the broader population by continuously analysing data. It is essential to identify any new risks associated with long-term use or interactions with other drugs.

However, integrating AI into pharmacovigilance can present challenges, such as ensuring data quality and privacy, addressing algorithm biases, and maintaining ethical and regulatory standards. Despite these challenges, the potential of AI to revolutionise pharmacovigilance is immense! It could offer a proactive approach to drug safety, leading to better patient care and improved public health outcomes.

Clinical Trial Matching

One of the most exciting applications of AI is clinical trial matching. With its powerful data processing and analytical capabilities, AI helps to match patients to the most suitable clinical trials accurately and efficiently.

It involves looking at each patient's unique medical profile, including diagnoses, medical history, genetic information, response to previous treatments, and lifestyle factors.

AI algorithms are good at sifting through extensive databases of ongoing clinical trials, each with specific inclusion and exclusion criteria. By meticulously comparing these criteria against detailed patient data, AI systems can identify matches with precision and detail that surpass traditional manual methods. It helps ensure that patients are matched with trials that are most likely to help them and for which they are eligible, thus improving the chances of successful treatment outcomes. And the best part? AI significantly speeds up the matching process!

It usually involves a lot of research and manual cross-referencing. But, with the help of AI, this process can be automated and streamlined, making it much faster and more efficient. It is especially critical for patients with conditions that require urgent treatment.

Moreover, AI allows broadening the scope of search and analysis in clinical trial matching. It considers a broader range of trials that might be typically missed in manual searches, including geographically distant but highly relevant or newly launched trials. This comprehensive approach allows every potentially beneficial trial to be noticed and explored.

By using AI to match patients to trials, we can gain valuable insights that can guide ongoing research and inform the design of future clinical trials. It can accelerate the development of new treatments and improve patient outcomes! However, we must prioritise data privacy and security when using AI in clinical trial matching.

We need to protect sensitive patient information and ensure the ethical use of AI algorithms. Moreover, it's crucial to maintain transparency in AI decision-making processes to ensure trust and reliability in these advanced systems. Overall, AI's role in clinical trial matching is a significant step forward in personalised medicine, and it's exciting to see how this technology can potentially transform healthcare for the better!

Patient Recruitment

NLP can identify patients for clinical trials based on their clinical notes. Did you know that patient recruitment is crucial in clinical trials? Well, it does! That's where Natural Language Processing (NLP) comes in handy.

We can easily extract, analyse, and interpret important information from various unstructured sources using NLP. This, in turn, helps us identify and recruit eligible participants for clinical trials.

NLP is a powerful AI tool that has completely changed how researchers work in biology and medicine. With NLP, researchers can easily extract information from scientific literature, saving time and effort.

By quickly and accurately analysing vast amounts of data, NLP helps researchers identify new targets for drug development and gain valuable insights into the underlying mechanisms of diseases.

The power of NLP is genuinely inspiring, and it's exciting to see how it's unlocking the secrets of biology and medicine.

Integrating Artificial Intelligence (AI) in healthcare has revolutionised how we recruit patients for clinical trials. With AI's advanced data analysis capabilities, we can make the recruitment process more efficient and effective.

By harnessing this technology, we can tackle the often-challenging task of identifying suitable candidates for clinical studies and positively impacting the future of healthcare.

Using AI, researchers can quickly identify potential candidates who meet specific criteria, ensuring that only suitable patients are approached for each study.

This targeted approach is much more accurate than traditional methods, and it helps to enrol patients who are most likely to benefit from and contribute valuable data to the trial. With AI's precision, we can ensure that clinical trials are more effective and efficient than ever!

Automating some initial screening and identification processes frees researchers and healthcare providers to focus on engaging with patients and enrolling them in the trial. It can benefit trials with specific eligibility criteria or those that need to register patients quickly.

By analysing patients' past behaviour and health data, AI systems can forecast which patients are more likely to stay committed to the study. It reduces dropout rates and ensures more reliable results.

Also, by tailoring information and interactions based on individual patient preferences and needs, AI-driven tools can create a better overall experience and increase participation rates.

AI can be an excellent tool for patient recruitment, but we must be careful about privacy, ethics, and consent. We must keep patient data protected and secure and be open and honest about using AI in the recruitment process. We also need to ensure that our AI algorithms are fair and unbiased to ensure we're not skewing our recruitment efforts.

AI helps with patient recruitment for clinical trials, making recruitment more efficient and effective. Plus, it has the potential to speed up the development of new medical treatments and therapies, which can lead to better patient outcomes and advancements in healthcare.

CHAPTER 9

MISUSE OF MEDICAL AI TOOLS AND RISKS

Knowing the potential risks associated with using Artificial Intelligence (AI) tools in healthcare is essential. Although AI can potentially transform healthcare for the better, it's necessary to use these tools properly.

Overreliance on AI systems without proper human oversight can lead to errors in diagnosis or treatment, so it's crucial to continuously evaluate and monitor AI-generated recommendations. Let's work together to ensure we use AI safely and effectively in healthcare.

One of the things we need to be mindful of when using AI systems in healthcare is the data quality and possible biases.

You see, the accuracy of an AI algorithm heavily relies on the data used to train it. If the data is complete, balanced, and of good quality, the AI's outputs may be accurate, resulting in correct diagnoses or treatment recommendations. It is particularly concerning when considering and representing diverse patient populations, which may worsen healthcare disparities.

It's important to remember that data privacy and security are paramount for AI systems in healthcare. These systems use a lot of personal health information, so it's crucial to keep that data secure and use it in compliance with privacy laws and ethical standards to ensure patient confidentiality is always protected.

Also, we must be careful with AI tools and ensure they're being used for their intended purposes and are correctly validated. Otherwise, we run the risk of getting inaccurate or misleading results. For example, we could have errors if we use an AI model developed for one disease or population in a different context without adjusting it. Let's ensure we use AI tools responsibly and with care for the best possible outcomes!

Another risk is that sometimes companies prioritise profit over patient care, leading to biased AI recommendations for specific drugs or treatments. Additionally, the rapid evolution of AI can sometimes outpace the development of appropriate regulatory frameworks, leading to a gap in oversight and quality assurance of AI tools in healthcare.

It's essential to remember that medical AI comes with some risks if not used properly, just like with any new technology. While the algorithms used in medical AI are highly accurate and reliable, their effectiveness depends mainly on how healthcare professionals and patients use them.

If not used correctly, it could lead to incorrect medical decisions and harm to the patient. Therefore, everyone needs to be well-informed about using medical AI tools.

It's not just about having access to these technologies but also knowing how and when to use them. In the coming years, AI-powered healthcare solutions must be flexible and adaptable. It means they must be designed to learn from new scenarios and mistakes as they arise in real-world settings.

However, this will require some human oversight to identify any issues. It may increase costs initially, but it's an essential step in ensuring AI is used safely and effectively in healthcare. To support this, we'll need to develop the necessary infrastructure and technology to facilitate regular AI updates.

We must implement policies that ensure these updates are integrated seamlessly into healthcare settings. I wanted to share some information about medical AI and how it could be misused and harm patients. One of the reasons for concern is the accessibility of medical AI applications, such as mobile apps, that can detect skin cancer by analysing a picture of your skin.

It's great that anyone can easily access these apps. But, sometimes, we need to learn how the AI algorithms have been developed and validated, and we're still determining their reliability and clinical efficacy.

That's why it's essential to use them with caution, and if you have any concerns about health issues, you should talk to a healthcare professional. Healthcare professionals, like doctors and nurses, follow specific guidelines and standards to provide the best care for their patients.

When artificial intelligence technology is introduced into their daily work, it can have practical, technical, and clinical implications that affect both them and their patients.

It's crucial for AI tools used in healthcare to be easy to integrate into existing clinical and technical workflows without making significant changes. This way, they can be used across different healthcare settings.

AI manufacturers, working with healthcare professionals and organisations, should establish standard procedures for new AI tools to ensure their compatibility with clinical sites and electronic healthcare systems.

This will help the AI tools to work seamlessly with other technologies, such as electronic patient records and health consultations, and not interfere with current practice models and training programs. By doing this, we can ensure that healthcare professionals can use AI tools to improve patient care safely and efficiently.

Future Research Directions:

AI has already made its way into the healthcare industry. It's impressive, but some things still need to be figured out before it can be used in clinical practice. Let's explore some details and prospects that need to be addressed.

Internet of Things:

Will the Internet of Things (IoT) play a vital role in providing healthcare services in the future? However, we must be cautious of cyber and physical attacks that can harm the infrastructure.

Malicious software like worms, viruses, and trojan horses can be risky for patients' health and privacy.

It's important to note that there have been recent concerns about the safety and security of our essential healthcare services.

We need to find ways to prevent any threats or interruptions from happening. Shortly, we expect to see more Internet of Things (IoT) devices that will likely be powered by the latest 5G and 6G mobile networks currently in development.

5G technology is a game-changer for the telecommunications industry. It can help solve many problems, expanding into new areas like cloud computing and smart devices. 5G and health monitoring are being integrated more and more these days. However, we should also be aware of the security implications of this trend and analyse them carefully.

Data sharing & efficiency:

To help more people through healthcare, we must share more data among stakeholders. However, some people are hesitant to share their data due to concerns about privacy and security. These are valid worries, and it's essential to address them to ensure everyone's peace of mind.

It's becoming increasingly crucial for the healthcare industry to understand the potential of big data and AI. With suitable applications, these technologies are incredibly useful in solving some of the industry's most significant challenges. However, it's important to note that not all problems require AI techniques - alternative approaches can be just as effective.

To address these risks, we must ensure that AI tools are rigorously validated and continuously monitored based on real-world performance. Maintaining strict data privacy and security standards and balancing AI assistance and human decision-making in healthcare is also essential.

Ultimately, we want to ensure that AI tools are used ethically and responsibly to benefit patient care and advance healthcare outcomes.

CHAPTER 10

INTRODUCTION TO AI IN SURGICAL ROBOTICS

Artificial Intelligence (AI) is transforming the way we approach healthcare. Surgical robotics is one of the most exciting areas where AI is making a significant impact. It's revolutionising the future of surgical procedures and enhancing patient outcomes. This subchapter will explore how AI and robotics work together to make surgery safer and more efficient.

AI in surgical robotics is an incredible field that aims to improve surgical precision, efficiency, and patient care. It combines the power of machine learning and robotics to assist surgeons in performing complex procedures with greater accuracy and minimal invasiveness.

Imagine how amazing it would be to have a robot that can help a surgeon perform delicate procedures with enhanced agility and control! This technology can potentially revolutionise how surgeries are performed, ultimately improving patient care.

One exciting application is image-guided surgery. AI algorithms are integrated with medical imaging techniques to give surgeons real-time, three-dimensional visualisations of the patient's anatomy. This enables them to plan and execute procedures with unparalleled precision.

Another area where AI is making significant strides is in robotic-assisted surgery. With AI-powered robots, surgeons can perform delicate procedures with enhanced agility and control, which is especially useful in complex surgeries where even the slightest error can have severe consequences.

AI in surgical robotics is making a significant impact on healthcare. With advanced AI algorithms, robots can analyse patient data, identify patterns, and make informed decisions in real time. This helps reduce the surgeon's workload and ensures consistent and standardised patient care.

Although it's important to note that AI in surgical robotics is not meant to replace human surgeons, it's a powerful tool that enhances their skills and expertise, enabling them to deliver better patient care. AI is transforming how surgeries are performed, enhancing precision, efficiency, and patient outcomes. By embracing this technology, surgeons can harness the power of AI to deliver better healthcare, ultimately improving patients' lives worldwide.

Understanding Surgical Robotics

Artificial intelligence (AI) has been brought into the operating room to help save lives and make surgeries more precise than ever before.

Let me explain the topic in more straightforward terms if you need to get more with the subject. Surgical robotics combines advanced robotic systems with AI algorithms to assist surgeons in performing precise and minimally invasive surgeries. By using AI, these robots can analyse vast amounts of data, make real-time decisions, and execute precise movements, sometimes surpassing human capabilities.

This technology is revolutionising the field of surgery by allowing for minimally invasive procedures, which means smaller incisions, less scarring, and faster patient recovery times.

The robots used in surgical robotics are equipped with small, flexible instruments that can manoeuvre through tight spaces with greater precision, leading to improved surgical outcomes. And that's not all - AI plays a crucial role in surgical robotics by providing intelligent automation. With the help of machine learning algorithms, the robots can learn from past surgical procedures, adapt to new situations, and continuously improve their performance. This allows surgeons to benefit from accumulated knowledge and experience, leading to better decision-making during complex surgeries.

In addition, AI-powered robots can offer steadiness and accuracy during complex surgeries by compensating for human hand tremors. Surgeons can also rely on haptic feedback systems that simulate the sense of touch, allowing them to feel the tissues remotely and perform delicate tasks with greater accuracy.

It's a fascinating field with so much potential, but there are also some essential challenges we need to address. For example, we must ensure that patient data is kept private, algorithms are easy to understand, and ethical guidelines are followed. This is crucial to maintaining trust in this technology and ensuring it benefits everyone.

At the same time, focusing on the many positive outcomes that AI in surgical robotics can offer is essential. With enhanced precision, minimally invasive procedures, and intelligent automation, we can achieve better surgical outcomes than ever before.

The Role of AI in Surgical Robotics

Artificial intelligence (AI) has emerged as a game-changer in various fields, and surgical robotics is one area where its impact is particularly significant. AI technology revolutionises surgeries, improving precision, efficiency, and patient outcomes. This subchapter will explore AI's crucial role in surgical robotics, focusing on its benefits and applications.

One of the critical advantages of AI in surgical robotics is its ability to enhance precision and accuracy. Surgeons can rely on AI-powered robots to perform intricate tasks with unparalleled precision, minimising the risk of human error.

These robots are equipped with advanced imaging and sensing technologies, allowing them to navigate through delicate tissues and perform complex procedures more accurately than traditional surgery. This level of precision translates into improved patient safety, reduced complications, and faster recovery times.

Another vital role of AI in surgical robotics is its capacity to automate repetitive and mundane tasks. By delegating routine tasks to robots, surgeons can focus on more critical aspects of the procedure, such as decision-making and delicate manoeuvres. AI algorithms enable robots to learn from past surgeries and adapt their techniques accordingly, leading to increased efficiency and better outcomes.

Furthermore, AI in surgical robotics enables real-time data analysis and decision support. Surgical robots can continuously monitor patients' vital signs, provide live feedback to surgeons, and alert them of any potential risks or complications.

AI algorithms can analyse vast amounts of patient data, helping surgeons make more informed decisions during surgeries. This advanced data-driven approach allows for personalised and targeted treatments, ultimately improving patient outcomes.

The applications of AI in surgical robotics are vast and diverse. It is used in minimally invasive surgeries, such as laparoscopy and robotic-assisted procedures, where precision and manoeuvrability are paramount. AI-powered robots can perform tasks like suturing, tissue manipulation, and organ retraction with remarkable skill and control.

Moreover, AI is also utilised in training and simulation, enabling surgeons to practice complex procedures in a virtual environment before performing them on actual patients.

In conclusion, AI is pivotal in advancing surgical robotics and automation. Its ability to enhance precision, automate tasks, provide real-time data analysis, and enable personalised treatments has transformed the field of surgery. As AI continues to evolve, we can expect even more groundbreaking advancements in surgical robotics, leading to safer, more efficient, and ultimately, better patient care.

Foundations of AI in Surgical Robotics

Artificial Intelligence (AI) is taking the lead in enhancing the capabilities of robotic systems. It's true! Surgeons and researchers use AI to improve surgical outcomes, minimise risks, and streamline the process.

Integrating AI into surgical robots allows these machines to analyse vast amounts of data, identify patterns, and make informed decisions in real time. This is particularly useful in assisting surgeons during complex procedures. AI algorithms can analyse medical images, like CT scans or MRIs, to identify abnormalities or potential areas of concern. This helps surgeons perform procedures more accurately and efficiently.

Another fantastic application of AI in surgical robotics is the ability to automate repetitive and mundane tasks. For example, AI-powered robotic arms can suture wounds or assist in removing tumours, reducing the strain on surgeons and improving overall surgical outcomes. AI algorithms can also monitor patients during surgery, analyse vital signs, and alert medical personnel of real-time anomalies.

However, it's important to note that AI in surgical robotics is not meant to replace human surgeons. Instead, it is designed to augment their skills and expertise, improve patient outcomes, and revolutionise surgery.

In conclusion, AI is a crucial component of surgical robotics and automation. By harnessing its power, surgical robots can analyse data, make informed decisions, and assist surgeons during complex procedures. AI in surgical robotics has the potential to transform the field of surgery, enhancing patient outcomes and revolutionising the way surgeries are performed. Exciting times ahead!

Machine Learning in Surgical Robotics

In recent years, surgical robotics has revolutionised by integrating artificial intelligence (AI) and machine learning techniques. These advances have paved the way for more precise, efficient, and safer surgical procedures. This subchapter aims to provide a comprehensive overview of machine learning in surgical robotics, catering specifically to a non-technical audience interested in the niches of AI in surgical robotics and automation.

It involves training algorithms to make decisions based on data. In surgical robotics, machine learning algorithms can analyse surgical data, including images, videos, and patient records, to extract valuable insights and improve surgical outcomes.

One of the critical applications of machine learning in surgical robotics is in surgical planning. By analysing preoperative images and patient data, machine learning algorithms can assist surgeons in creating personalised surgical plans.

These plans consider individual patient characteristics, allowing for more accurate and efficient procedures. This reduces the risk of complications and minimises the overall time spent in the operating room.

Surgeons can now access real-time data from sensors and cameras thanks to surgical robots with advanced machine-learning algorithms. This helps them gain valuable insights and guidance during procedures, leading to better decision-making and patient outcomes. With the help of this technology, surgeons can navigate complex anatomical structures, avoid vital structures, and optimise surgical techniques.

Machine learning is vital in postoperative care and recovery. Machine learning algorithms can detect early signs of complications or adverse events by analysing patient data and monitoring vital signs. This helps healthcare providers intervene promptly and prevent potential complications, ensuring patient recovery.

Machine learning in surgical robotics isn't meant to replace human surgeons. Instead, it's designed to augment their capabilities and provide valuable assistance and insights. Surgeons remain in control throughout the procedure, with machine learning algorithms giving support.

In conclusion, integrating machine learning in surgical robotics has revolutionised the field, enhancing surgical planning, assisting surgeons during procedures, and improving postoperative care. These advancements in AI have paved the way for more precise, efficient, and safer surgical interventions. As the field continues to evolve, machine learning will undoubtedly play a central role in shaping the future of surgical robotics, ultimately benefiting patients and healthcare providers alike.

Deep Learning and Neural Networks in Surgical Robotics

These innovative technologies have revolutionised surgical procedures, making them more precise, efficient, and safe for patients. This subchapter will explore the profound impact of deep learning and neural networks in AI-driven surgical robotics. Don't worry; we'll keep things easy to understand even if you're not a technical expert.

Deep learning, a part of AI, is used in surgical robotics. It involves teaching artificial neural networks to recognise patterns and make decisions based on vast data. Deep learning models can identify intricate patterns and gain valuable insights by analysing surgical data, including images, videos, and patient records. This can help surgeons make more accurate diagnoses and perform surgeries precisely.

Using cameras and sensors, these models can analyse the surgical field, identify anatomical structures, and provide real-time guidance to surgeons. This helps them navigate through delicate tissues and avoid critical structures, ultimately reducing the risk of complications and improving patient outcomes.

Neural networks play a crucial role in surgical automation, allowing robotic systems to learn from past surgeries and adjust their movements accordingly.

This means that robots can now handle routine tasks with minimal human intervention, leaving the surgeons free to concentrate on the more complex aspects of the procedure. The best part is that neural networks can continue to learn and improve over time, making surgical robots even more advanced and capable.

With the help of deep learning and neural networks, surgeons are now equipped with AI-driven tools that make surgeries more precise, efficient, and safe for patients. I'm amazed at how these technologies have enabled real-time guidance, surgical automation, and image recognition.

As AI continues to evolve, I'm excited to see what the future holds for surgical robotics. It's great to know that these advancements in medical practices will ultimately benefit both patients and healthcare providers.

Preoperative Planning and Simulation

AI is playing a crucial role in surgical robotics and automation. One of the ways it is doing this is by revolutionising the preoperative planning process. This is where a doctor assesses a patient's condition and creates a detailed surgical plan well before the procedure occurs. With the help of AI-powered tools and technologies, doctors can now make more informed decisions, leading to better patient outcomes.

One of the most crucial parts of this planning process is using medical imaging techniques like computed tomography (CT), magnetic resonance imaging (MRI), and ultrasound. These scans give your doctor a detailed, three-dimensional view of your body to identify potential challenges and plan the best approach for your surgery. By doing this, they can also determine the ideal placement of robotic surgical instruments. It might sound complicated, but it's an important step to ensure your surgery goes smoothly.

Artificial intelligence algorithms are helping surgeons process and analyse large amounts of medical imaging data. This allows them to simulate surgeries beforehand and improve patient outcomes. And with the help of virtual and augmented reality technologies, surgeons can even practice complex procedures in a risk-free environment! It's incredible how technology advances to make medical procedures safer and more effective.

Preoperative simulation is a highly effective technique that helps surgeons prepare for surgeries by simulating them in advance. This technique enables them to identify potential complications, devise contingency plans, and enhance their understanding of the patient's anatomy. In addition, preoperative simulation helps in training surgical teams, ensuring that everyone involved in the procedure is well-prepared and aware of their roles and responsibilities.

Another remarkable advantage of using AI in surgery is that it can analyse vast patient data, including medical records, previous surgical outcomes, and even real-time patient monitoring. This data-driven approach allows surgeons to make evidence-based decisions, which enhances the precision and safety of surgeries. With the help of AI, surgeons can perform surgeries with greater accuracy and efficiency, ultimately leading to better patient outcomes.

Surgeons can visualise, simulate, and strategise their surgeries with unprecedented accuracy using AI's preoperative planning and simulation tools, leading to better patient outcomes and reduced surgical risks.

Robot-assisted and Image-Guided Surgery

One of the most exciting developments is robot-assisted surgery. This incredible technique combines the accuracy of artificial intelligence (AI) with the skill of surgeons. In this section, we'll explore the fascinating world of robot-assisted surgery.

It involves using robots with advanced AI algorithms to help surgeons perform complex procedures with greater precision and control. These robots work alongside surgeons to perform minimally invasive surgeries, improving patient outcomes. By providing surgeons with a clear, magnified view of the surgical site, robot-assisted surgery helps ensure that every movement is precise and accurate.

It's that it's much less invasive than traditional open surgeries. With robot-assisted surgery, smaller incisions are made, which means less pain, less blood loss, and less scarring. Because of this, patients usually have shorter hospital stays and recover faster, so they can return to their daily routines sooner. It's a real game-changer in the field of medicine!

By integrating AI technology, surgeons can now automate specific tasks and make better decisions during surgeries. This is because AI algorithms can analyse a vast amount of patient data, which helps surgeons make more informed decisions during operations. Plus, with real-time monitoring and feedback, surgeons can get alerts about potential complications or issues during the procedure. Robot-assisted surgery is more efficient and safer for patients since it minimises errors and ensures optimal outcomes.

Not only does this technology have the potential to make surgeries more efficient, but it could also lessen the workload on surgeons, giving them more time to focus on complex cases.

Robot-assisted surgery presents a range of benefits, like improved precision, less invasiveness, and better patient outcomes. With technology constantly improving, there's much excitement about AI's possibilities for the future of surgical procedures. By learning to operate these machines, surgeons can use AI to overcome limitations and take on new challenges in surgery, ultimately leading to better healthcare for everyone.

These technologies have made considerable strides in recent years, especially with the integration of artificial intelligence (AI). One of the most significant advancements is image-guided surgery, changing the game for complex procedures.

Image-guided surgery, also known as computer-assisted or navigated surgery, uses AI algorithms and high-resolution imaging to provide real-time guidance to surgeons during operations. This technology enhances precision, accuracy, and safety, ultimately improving patient outcomes.

It involves merging preoperative imaging data like CT scans or MRI with the patient's anatomy during the surgery. This integration enables surgeons to better understand the patient's internal structures with greater precision, assisting them in planning their approach and performing the surgery more confidently.

Image-guided surgery is a fantastic technology that has numerous benefits. Firstly, it helps surgeons identify critical structures, like blood vessels or nerves, that might be hidden or challenging to locate during traditional surgery. This helps them avoid any potential complications and reduce damage to healthy tissues.

Moreover, image-guided surgery enables surgeons to target tumours or lesions precisely, making removing diseased tissue easier while sparing healthy areas. This level of accuracy is fundamental in delicate procedures, such as brain or spinal surgeries, where even a slight deviation can have serious consequences.

Another great thing about image-guided surgery is that it provides real-time feedback to the surgeon throughout the procedure, allowing for dynamic adjustments and ensuring the best possible outcome.

By continuously updating the virtual model with the patient's current anatomy, surgeons can adapt their approach as needed, enhancing accuracy and minimising the risk of errors.

And the integration of AI technology in image-guided surgery is also very promising. Machine learning algorithms can analyse vast amounts of data from previous surgeries and provide surgeons with predictive insights, helping them make informed decisions and improving patient outcomes.

In conclusion, image-guided surgery significantly advances AI in surgical robotics and automation. By leveraging the power of AI algorithms and high-resolution imaging, surgeons can perform procedures with unprecedented precision, accuracy, and safety.

Reduced Human Error and Fatigue

One of the most significant benefits of incorporating AI in surgical robotics and automation is the potential to reduce human error and fatigue during complex surgical procedures. Traditional surgical techniques heavily rely on human skill and concentration, which can lead to mistakes due to fatigue, stress, or distractions. However, these limitations can be mitigated with AI technology, leading to improved patient outcomes and safer surgical practices.

AI-powered surgical robots can perform precise and repetitive tasks with unparalleled accuracy. These robots have advanced sensors and imaging technologies to navigate and interact with human anatomy in real time. By leveraging machine learning algorithms, these systems can learn from vast amounts of data, including medical images, patient records, and surgical techniques, to assist surgeons during complex procedures.

One of the primary advantages of AI in surgical robotics is reducing human error. Surgeons, no matter how skilled, are still susceptible to making mistakes. Fatigue, stress, and distractions during long surgeries can compromise their decision-making abilities and hand-eye coordination. In contrast, AI-powered robotic systems are not prone to such limitations. They do not experience fatigue, and their algorithms are designed to consistently make accurate assessments and decisions based on the available data.

Additionally, AI in surgical robotics can help address human limitations related to hand trembling, which can be particularly crucial in delicate procedures. Robotic systems can enhance precision and minimise the risk of accidental tissue damage by stabilising the surgeon's movements and filtering out unwanted tremors.

By reducing human error and fatigue, AI in surgical robotics ultimately enhances patient safety. Surgeons can rely on these intelligent systems to aid, guide, and even perform specific tasks autonomously. This collaborative approach between human surgeons and AI-powered robots maximises the benefits of both expertise, resulting in more efficient surgeries and improved patient outcomes.

In conclusion, integrating AI in surgical robotics and automation holds immense potential for reducing human error and fatigue during complex medical procedures. By leveraging machine learning algorithms, AI-powered robotic systems can enhance surgical precision, minimise the risk of mistakes, and improve patient safety.

This technology empowers surgeons with invaluable assistance and guidance, leading to more effective surgeries and better patient outcomes. With continued advancements in AI and surgical robotics, the future of surgery looks promising, with increased reliance on intelligent machines to support and augment human expertise in the operating room.

Ethical and Legal Considerations

With the exciting advancements in AI-powered surgical robotics and automation, it's essential that we also take the time to consider the ethical and legal implications that come with these developments. As we continue integrating artificial intelligence into surgical procedures, we must do so responsibly and with the well-being of patients and society in mind.

While AI in surgical robotics can be a game-changer in improving surgical outcomes and reducing human error, we also need to be mindful of the potential risks and challenges that come with it. One critical consideration is patient safety. We need to establish robust safety protocols and regulations to ensure that patients are not at risk.

We also need transparency in developing and testing these AI systems, ensuring they are thoroughly evaluated for safety and effectiveness before being used on patients. By taking these steps, we can ensure that AI in surgical robotics is used in patients' best interests.

AI algorithms can sometimes have biases. This is because they are trained on large datasets that may contain biases that can lead to unequal treatment or outcomes for different groups of people. But don't worry; there are ways to address and mitigate these biases. By collecting data carefully and developing algorithms thoughtfully, we can ensure that everyone is treated fairly. It's also essential to involve diverse experts in the development process to help identify and rectify any potential biases.

Using AI in surgical robotics raises legal and ethical concerns about accountability and liability. In cases where autonomous systems are used, it is necessary to determine who is responsible in the event of system failure or adverse outcome. Clear legal frameworks and guidelines must be established to ensure the safety and security of patients. In the event of harm caused by AI systems, assigning liability and providing patients with recourse is crucial.

Another critical consideration of AI in surgical robotics is protecting patient data and privacy. These systems rely on extensive data collection and analysis to function, making it essential to have strong data protection measures to safeguard patient information. Compliance with data protection regulations and obtaining informed consent from patients are paramount to maintaining trust and protecting patient privacy.

Keeping ethics and law in mind when using robots and automation in surgery is essential. By doing this, we can ensure that patients are safe, things are fair, and everyone is held accountable. Suppose we work together and keep talking about these topics. In that case, we can create guidelines and rules that help us use this unique technology responsibly and ethically.

Ensuring Regulatory Compliance

When using AI in surgical robotics, we must follow the rules. We must use AI responsibly and ethically while meeting regulatory guidelines to keep our patients safe. Regulatory compliance means following the standards set by organisations like the FDA in the US and the EMA in Europe. These regulations help ensure that the AI systems we use in surgical robotics are trustworthy, effective, and, most importantly, safe for everyone involved.

If you're using AI to build something, it's essential to ensure it's safe. To do that, you must test it carefully and ensure it does what it should. This will help you ensure it is reliable and won't cause any harm. This involves assessing the accuracy and reliability of your AI algorithms, testing their performance in different scenarios, and identifying any potential risks or limitations.

After you feel confident that your AI-powered surgical robotics technology is performing well, the next step is to get regulatory approval or clearance. This involves providing detailed documentation that describes the process of designing, developing, testing and intended use of your system. The regulatory authorities will review your documentation to ensure your technology is safe and effective and meets all the relevant regulations.

It's important to remember that more than obtaining regulatory approval for AI-powered surgical robotics is needed. We must also ensure the technology is constantly monitored to perform safely and effectively in real-world clinical settings. This means regularly analysing data, conducting audits, and reporting any issues.

It's also essential to remember that regulations can change as technology evolves. Hence, developers and healthcare professionals must stay current and ensure their AI systems remain compliant. By prioritising regulatory compliance, we can continue to advance AI in surgical robotics safely and responsibly, giving patients the best care possible while building trust in the technology.

Overcoming Cost Challenges

In the fast-evolving field of AI in surgical robotics and automation, one of the significant obstacles that organisations face is the high costs associated with implementing these technologies. However, with strategic planning and innovative approaches, overcoming these cost challenges and reaping the benefits of AI-driven surgical robotics is possible.

1. Collaboration and Partnerships:

Collaborating with industry leaders, healthcare providers, and technology companies can help bridge the cost gap. Organisations can reduce costs by pooling resources, sharing knowledge, and leveraging existing infrastructure while embracing AI in surgical robotics.

2. Scalability and Flexibility:

Designing scalable and adaptable systems can significantly impact costs. By developing platforms that can be easily integrated into existing surgical infrastructure, organisations can avoid the need for expensive retrofitting or complete system replacements.

3. Modular Approach:

Adopting a modular approach to AI in surgical robotics allows organisations to focus on specific areas that require automation rather than implementing complex and costly systems across the board. This targeted approach ensures that resources are utilised efficiently, reducing overall costs.

4. Training and Education:

Investing in training programs for surgeons, technicians, and other healthcare professionals is crucial for successful implementation. By educating the workforce on the benefits and intricacies of AI in surgical robotics, organisations can optimise the utilisation of these technologies, leading to improved patient outcomes and cost savings in the long run.

5. Value-based Purchasing:

Adopting a value-based purchasing model encourages organisations to prioritise the long-term benefits and outcomes of AI-driven surgical robotics over the immediate costs. Organisations can justify the initial expenses by evaluating the return on investment based on patient outcomes and efficiency gains.

6. Regulatory and Reimbursement Support:

Advocating for favourable regulatory frameworks and reimbursement policies can alleviate some financial burdens associated with AI in surgical robotics. Engaging with policymakers and payers to highlight the potential cost savings and patient benefits can lead to improved funding options and accelerated adoption.

7. Research and Development Collaboration:

Collaborating with universities, research institutions, and government agencies can provide access to grants, funding, and shared resources. This collaborative approach reduces costs, fosters innovation, and accelerates the development of AI-driven technologies in surgical robotics.

We are looking to make AI-driven surgical robotics more cost-effective. In that case, there are some key strategies we can consider. Collaboration, scalability, targeted implementation, education, value-based purchasing, policy advocacy, and research collaboration are all critical approaches. By adopting these strategies, organisations can navigate the financial barriers and unlock the transformative potential of AI in surgical robotics. This not only improves patient care but also optimises costs.

In recent years, surgical robotics has witnessed an unprecedented revolution. With the advent of Artificial Intelligence (AI), surgeons can now perform complex procedures with greater precision, efficiency, and safety. However, this rapid technological advancement has also created a gap between surgeons and the tools they rely on.

This field is full of potential, where intelligent algorithms and robotic systems work together with surgeons to help achieve better patient outcomes. But we know all the technical jargon can be overwhelming sometimes. We've compiled this easy-to-understand subchapter to demystify the concepts and explain how AI can benefit surgeons and patients.

With the help of surgical robots equipped with AI algorithms, surgeons can get real-time feedback and make informed decisions that lead to better outcomes and faster patient recovery. By working hand in hand with technology, AI bridges the gap between surgeons and the latest advancements, ensuring that surgeries are optimised and patients stay safe.

Despite the highest level of expertise, human error remains a concern in complex surgeries. AI can act as a safety net by continuously monitoring vital signs, analysing patient data, and alerting surgeons to potential risks. By augmenting surgical skills, AI helps minimise errors, improve patient safety, and enhance surgical outcomes.

AI-powered simulators enable surgeons to practice procedures in a risk-free virtual environment, enhancing their skills and confidence. Surgeons can gain valuable experience, refine their techniques, and explore innovative approaches through realistic simulations.

Integrating AI into surgical training benefits surgeons and ensures patients receive the highest standard of care.

By providing a comprehensive overview of how AI enhances surgical precision, reduces errors, and improves training, we aim to empower non-technical individuals to understand and appreciate the profound impact of AI on the future of surgery. With AI bridging the gap between surgeons and technology, we are witnessing a new era in surgical robotics that holds tremendous promise for advancing patient care.

Potential Risks and Failures

The field of AI in surgical robotics and automation is changing rapidly, and it's essential to understand the potential risks and challenges that come with it. Although AI can potentially improve surgical outcomes and revolutionise healthcare, it has challenges. There are some potential risks and challenges to implementing AI in surgical robotics.

We need to remember the possibility of errors or malfunctions in the AI system. Although AI algorithms are designed to be accurate and efficient, there is always a chance of a hiccup or a bug that could result in incorrect decisions or actions during surgery. This could affect the patient's safety and the surgery's outcome. That's why it's important to continually test, monitor, and update the system to minimise any risks.

Sometimes, algorithms can be unintentionally biased because they're trained on large datasets that may only be fully representative of some different types of people. This can lead to less accurate decision-making for patients from diverse backgrounds. So, we must recognise and address any potential bias in AI algorithms to ensure everyone receives fair and equal treatment regarding surgical robotics and automation.

In AI technology, there is a growing concern about the possibility of cyber-attacks and data breaches. As AI systems become more interconnected and rely on data exchange, they could become vulnerable to unauthorised access and hacking. This could compromise patient privacy, lead to manipulation of surgical procedures, or even result in ransomware attacks. However, there are ways to mitigate these risks! We can keep our systems safe and secure by implementing stringent security measures, encryption protocols, and constant monitoring.

Another crucial thing we must consider while using AI in surgical robotics is its ethical implications. It's essential to think about informed consent, transparency, and accountability when AI systems make decisions during surgery. Healthcare professionals and policymakers must navigate these ethical dilemmas with utmost care while keeping in mind the rights and autonomy of patients.

To sum it up, AI has the potential to bring about tremendous advancements in surgical robotics and automation. However, it's essential to remember that there may be risks and failures associated with AI implementation. We can work together to minimise errors, tackle bias, enhance cybersecurity, and address ethical concerns to fully leverage AI's benefits in surgical robotics. This will significantly benefit patients and transform the field of medicine as we know it.

Recommendations for Surgeons and Healthcare Professionals

As technology advances, healthcare professionals and surgeons must keep up with the latest developments in AI-powered surgical robotics. This section is here to help non-technical individuals in the industry by providing recommendations, insights, and guidance on effectively utilising surgical robotics.

1. Continuous Education:

Surgeons and healthcare professionals must commit to lifelong learning to stay at the forefront of AI in surgical robotics. Attend seminars, conferences, and workshops on AI and surgical robotics to learn about the latest developments, best practices, and emerging trends. Engage in online courses and certifications to enhance your skills and understanding of AI technologies.

2. Collaborative Approach:

Embrace a collaborative mindset by engaging with AI experts, engineers, and data scientists. Foster interdisciplinary collaborations to harness the power of AI in surgical robotics. Work together to understand the possibilities and limitations of AI technologies, ensuring safe and effective integration into surgical practices.

3. Ethical Considerations:

As AI becomes more prominent in surgical robotics, it is crucial to address the ethical aspects. Recognise and understand the ethical challenges associated with AI, such as data privacy, bias, and accountability. Engage in discussions and contribute to developing ethical guidelines that prioritise patient safety and well-being.

4. Data Management and Analysis:

AI in surgical robotics relies heavily on data. Surgeons and healthcare professionals must ensure proper data management, including collection, storage, and analysis. Collaborate with data scientists to use AI algorithms to analyse datasets effectively, extracting valuable insights to improve surgical outcomes.

5. Training and Simulation: Utilise

AI-powered training and simulation tools to enhance surgical skills and techniques. Virtual and augmented reality simulations can provide surgeons a safe and controlled environment to refine their skills and gain experience. Embrace these technologies to improve surgical precision and reduce risks.

6. Embrace Change:

AI in surgical robotics is transforming how surgeries are performed. Embrace this change and be open to adopting new technologies to enhance patient care. Emphasise the importance of ongoing evaluation and feedback to identify areas of improvement and refine the integration of AI in surgical practices.

The tips we've shared in this section are meant to help surgeons and healthcare professionals make the most of AI in surgical robotics. By staying curious, seeking expert advice, thinking about ethics, organising data effectively, using training and simulation resources, and keeping an open mind, they can harness the power of AI technologies to transform surgical procedures and enhance patient results.

How AI can help reduce waste in healthcare

To delve deeper into how AI can help reduce waste in healthcare, let's break down the key areas, exploring specific applications, benefits, and considerations in each domain. Optimising Resource Allocation:

Patient Flow Optimisation:

AI algorithms can forecast patient admissions and discharges, allowing hospitals to manage staffing levels, reduce bottlenecks, and allocate resources like beds and operating rooms more efficiently.

Also, by predicting peak times and patient influx, AI helps staff emergency rooms more effectively, reducing wait times and improving patient outcomes.

Inventory Management:

AI systems can predict the demand for different supplies and medications, automate restocking orders, and identify the most cost-effective suppliers, reducing excess inventory and ensuring the availability of necessary items.

Enhancing Diagnostic Accuracy:

AI algorithms excel at analysing images, such as X-rays, MRIs, and pathology slides, identifying patterns that the human eye might miss. It can lead to earlier detection of conditions like cancer, heart disease, and more.

Through the analysis of genetic data, AI can detect individuals who may be at a greater risk for specific diseases, which could help in taking early preventive measures and implementing personalised treatment plans.

AI can assist physicians in making diagnoses, offering additional opinions, reducing the chances of incorrect diagnoses, and ensuring that patients receive the necessary care.

Streamlining Administrative Processes:

Automated Paperwork can be achieved by utilising Natural Language Processing (NLP). AI-powered NLP can understand and organise unstructured medical records, automate coding for insurance claims, and even analyse clinical notes, reducing errors and saving time.

AI can predict no-shows and optimise appointment scheduling, ensuring that healthcare practitioners use time efficiently.

Fraud Detection:

AI systems can analyse billing patterns, identify unusual claims or billing practices, and flag these for further investigation, reducing fraudulent activities and ensuring appropriate use of resources.

Personalising Treatment:

By Integrating AI with patient data and current medical knowledge, these systems can suggest the most effective treatment plans, reducing the trial-and-error approach often associated with complex conditions.

AI can continuously analyse patient data to track the effectiveness of treatment, adjusting as necessary to improve outcomes.

Virtual Health Assistants:

AI-powered apps and devices can remind patients to take medications, track their symptoms, and even alert healthcare providers if a patient's condition worsens, reducing the need for in-person visits and interventions.

Improving Pharmaceutical Supply Chains:

AI can analyse vast datasets to identify potential drug candidates more quickly than traditional methods. AI can help design more efficient clinical trials, identifying suitable candidates and predicting outcomes, thus reducing the resources required for drug development.

Pharmaceutical Logistics:

AI can predict regional demand for various medications, optimise distribution networks, and reduce waste due to expiration or overstocking.

Enhancing Patient Engagement and Compliance:

AI can analyse patient behaviour and lifestyle data, tailoring health plans that are more likely to be followed and thus more effective. AI-driven platforms can provide personalised advice, motivate patients, and track progress, ensuring higher adherence to prescribed treatments and preventive measures.

Continuous Monitoring:

Devices equipped with AI can monitor vital signs, activity levels, and other health metrics in real-time, providing data that can be used to adjust treatments promptly and prevent acute episodes.

Challenges and Considerations:

AI in healthcare raises significant ethical questions about consent, privacy, and the potential for bias in treatment recommendations. For AI to be most effective, it must work seamlessly with various healthcare systems and technologies, which requires standardisation and interoperability.

The introduction of AI will change the nature of work in healthcare, requiring new skills and potentially displacing certain types of jobs, necessitating careful planning and retraining efforts.

In summary, AI offers a promising pathway to reduce waste across many aspects of healthcare, from clinical to operational to administrative. However, realising these benefits requires addressing significant challenges, including data management, system integration, ethical considerations, and ensuring that AI applications are designed and implemented to enhance patient care and system efficiency. With careful implementation and ongoing evaluation, AI can create a more efficient, effective, and patient-centred healthcare system.

MYTHS AND REALITIES OF AI IN HEALTHCARE

Artificial Intelligence (AI) in healthcare is a burgeoning field that promises to revolutionise medical practices and patient experiences. As with any emerging technology, it's accompanied by hype, hope, and concern. Let's examine some of the most common myths surrounding AI in healthcare, contrasting them with the realities to provide a nuanced understanding of this complex landscape.

Myth: AI Will Replace Human Physicians

The myth that AI will replace human physicians is rooted in the idea that technology will outpace human skills in accuracy, speed, and efficiency. Visions of AI doctors performing surgeries, making diagnoses, and providing patient care without human intervention are prevalent in popular media and discussions.

Reality Detail:

While AI has made significant strides in diagnostic accuracy and treatment recommendations, it needs more human doctors' nuanced understanding and emotional intelligence. AI is a tool designed to augment the capabilities of healthcare professionals, not replace them. It can sift through vast datasets, recognise patterns, and provide recommendations but cannot replicate human care's empathetic and ethical dimensions.

Moreover, the patient-doctor relationship is fundamental to healing and involves trust, empathy, and communication—qualities AI cannot emulate.

Myth: AI is Always Accurate

There's a common misconception that AI, with its data-driven approach, is inherently more objective and accurate than humans. This myth is predicated on the belief that AI eliminates human error and bias, leading to flawless diagnoses and treatment plans.

Myth: AI Can Fully Automate Patient Care

Another prevailing myth is that AI can take over all aspects of patient care, leading to fully automated healthcare systems. Proponents envision a future where robots and AI systems handle everything from diagnosis to treatment, minimising the need for human healthcare workers.

Reality Detail:

The reality is that patient care is an inherently complex and multifaceted endeavour that involves technical and medical skills, interpersonal communication, ethical decision-making, and emotional support. While AI can automate specific tasks, such as data analysis, appointment scheduling, and even some elements of diagnosis and monitoring, it cannot replace the human aspects of care.

Interactions between patients and healthcare providers are critical to understanding and addressing health concerns. AI is best viewed as a tool that supports and enhances the work of healthcare professionals, improving efficiency and accuracy but continually operating within a framework of human oversight and empathy.

Embracing the Realities and Addressing Challenges

As we navigate the myths and realities of AI in healthcare, it's crucial to address the challenges and ethical considerations that arise. Ensuring data privacy, security, and ethical use of AI is paramount. Healthcare providers, patients, and policymakers must work together to establish guidelines and standards for the safe and equitable use of AI in healthcare. It includes addressing data biases, ensuring transparency in AI algorithms, and fostering an informed and educated workforce capable of working alongside AI technologies.

The potential of AI is greatly restricted by inconsistencies in the availability and quality of digital data, as well as the need for significant computing power to analyse large and complex data sets. Despite enthusiasm for the possible uses of AI in the NHS, practical challenges such as inconsistent digitisation of medical records, lack of interoperability and standardisation in NHS IT systems, digital record-keeping, and data labelling must be addressed. Moreover, concerns about the digital sharing of personal health data by patients and doctors must be acknowledged and resolved.

It is a fact that AI systems may not be able to possess specific attributes that are unique to humans, such as compassion. Despite advancements in AI technology, there are still complex judgments and abilities in clinical practice that only humans can perform, such as contextual knowledge and the ability to read social cues. There is a debate about whether machines can teach humans tacit understanding. Some argue that machines display autonomy, but this idea is contested. Autonomy is a fundamental human characteristic and cannot be defined in the context of machines.

AI and technology can bring up some ethical and social issues that we must be aware of. These issues are closely related to how we use data, automation, and other technologies. We must also be careful when using assistive technologies and telehealth, as they pose significant challenges. So, we must address these concerns proactively to ensure that AI and technology are used in everyone's best interest ethically and responsibly.

It is essential to recognise that while AI-powered systems can be incredibly useful in controlling equipment, delivering treatment, or making healthcare decisions, their reliability and safety should never be taken for granted. Like any technology, AI systems are susceptible to errors, and if left undetected, these could have serious consequences. For example, in a clinical trial conducted in 2015, an AI app was utilised to predict which patients were likely to develop complications following pneumonia and required hospitalisation. It is, therefore, crucial to ensure that AI systems undergo rigorous testing, monitoring, and regulation to minimise the risk of errors and ensure their safety.

Many AI symptom checker apps have been questioned due to their unreliable performance. For instance, one such app mistakenly advised doctors to discharge asthma patients because it failed to consider contextual information. Additionally, the recommendations made by these apps are often overly cautious and may even lead to increased demand for unnecessary tests and treatments.

It is an undeniable fact that determining the underlying logic behind AI-generated outputs can be an arduous, if not impossible, task. While some AI technologies are proprietary and kept under wraps, others are so intricate that comprehending them is beyond human capability. In particular, Machine-learning systems can be highly opaque due to the constant adjustments of their parameters and rules as they learn. It presents a significant challenge when validating AI-generated outputs and detecting any errors or biases in the data.

Conclusion

Sometimes, people get scared or misunderstand what AI is capable of, thinking it's a magic solution for everything. But in reality, AI has the potential to enhance healthcare while still significantly requiring human expertise and care. It's not about replacing humans but about working together to achieve better patient outcomes and more personalised care. As we continue exploring and incorporating AI into healthcare, let's take a balanced, informed, and ethical approach to reap the benefits while minimising the risks.

CHAPTER 11

WHAT DOES THE
FUTURE HOLD?

The Future of AI In Healthcare

Artificial Intelligence (AI) will play a significant role in transforming the sector. With the advancements in AI technologies, patient care, diagnostics, treatment, and health management will significantly improve. AI will help us tackle complex challenges and make healthcare even better than before.

By analysing individual patient data, including genetics, lifestyle, and environmental factors, AI can help facilitate more effective and tailored therapies, particularly for chronic diseases and cancer. This precision approach could make a real difference in improving treatment outcomes and patient well-being.

With incredible advancements in machine learning and pattern recognition, AI will help us diagnose diseases faster and more accurately. Even complex conditions like neurological disorders and various forms of cancer will be easier to analyse with the help of AI. AI-driven image analysis in radiology and pathology is already showing great promise! These developments could lead to earlier detection of diseases, which will help us to treat them more effectively.

AI can help reduce wait times and improve patient care by automating administrative processes in hospitals and clinics. In addition, AI-powered telemedicine and diagnostic tools can provide critical healthcare services to remote or underserved areas, enhancing access for populations without adequate care.

Analysing massive clinical trials and research data can uncover new treatments and drug interactions. It means we could see more efficient drug development processes and faster introduction of new treatments!

Even more exciting is that AI is set to improve public health monitoring and response. With the help of AI, we can predict and manage epidemics more effectively and make informed public health decisions.

While there's much potential for exciting advancements in patient care, diagnostics, efficiency, and medical research, some challenges must be addressed. These include ensuring patient data stays private, minimising biases in AI algorithms, maintaining ethical standards, and ensuring that different AI systems can work together across other healthcare platforms.

AI is making a significant contribution to the healthcare industry by advancing the development of precision medicine through machine learning.

Although there have been some challenges in diagnosis and treatment recommendations, we are optimistic that AI will continue to make strides in these areas.

AI's rapid progress in imaging analysis suggests that machines will soon be able to examine most radiology and pathology images.

Furthermore, speech and text recognition technologies are already being used to facilitate patient communication and capture clinical notes, and these uses are expected to grow. However, the biggest challenge to AI in healthcare is ensuring its widespread adoption in clinical practice.

For this to happen, regulators must approve AI systems, integrate them with electronic health record systems, standardise them to ensure consistency, teach them to clinicians, fund them from public or private payers, and update them over time. While most of these challenges will eventually be overcome, it will take time.

It is worth noting that AI systems will not replace human clinicians but augment their work. As healthcare technology advances, clinicians can focus more on their human skills, such as empathy, persuasion, and big-picture thinking, enabling them to play an even more vital role in patient care.

Over time, clinicians may shift towards tasks that require more uniquely human skills, while AI takes on more routine and repetitive tasks. The fear of job losses due to the implementation of artificial intelligence (AI) in healthcare is a common concern and part of a broader discussion about the impact of automation on various industries.

However, it's understandable that introducing AI technologies may raise concerns about job displacement.

Job Transformation

While specific routine and repetitive tasks may be automated, the introduction of AI in healthcare is more likely to lead to a transformation of jobs rather than wholesale job losses. Healthcare professionals may work alongside AI systems, focusing more on tasks that require empathy, critical thinking, and complex decision-making.

AI is revolutionising job roles, responsibilities, and skill requirements across various positions. But don't worry, AI is not here to replace human workers; instead, it is a tool to enhance and augment their existing roles.

AI can significantly help medical professionals like doctors, nurses, and clinicians. With its advanced algorithms, AI can quickly analyse complex medical data, providing valuable insights that can assist in accurate diagnosis and personalised treatment planning. By automating routine tasks, AI can free healthcare professionals to focus more on patient care.

AI is already making a massive difference in the field of medical imaging. Radiologists and pathologists are seeing their jobs change as AI tools better analyse images for things like cancer. It's astonishing how these professionals now get to work closely with AI systems, interpreting their results and making sure everything is accurate. Overall, it's fantastic to see how AI is transforming how we approach healthcare!

With the rise of AI, many new job opportunities are being created in the healthcare field. For example, there is a growing need for data scientists and AI specialists to develop and manage AI applications in healthcare. Some roles focus on AI's ethical, legal, and social implications in healthcare that are becoming increasingly important. Seeing how AI transforms the healthcare industry and opens new possibilities is exciting!

Healthcare administrators and managers are also benefiting from the AI revolution. AI can optimise hospital operations, from scheduling appointments to managing patient flow and predicting hospital admission rates. Administrators can improve efficiency and patient services by integrating these new tools into their management strategies.

However, integrating AI requires a focus on continuous education and training for healthcare professionals. It's essential to stay updated with the latest developments and learn how to interact with AI systems effectively.

AI is helping us improve patient care and streamline operations, but it's also creating new job opportunities that require us to learn new skills and approaches. To ensure we keep putting patients first, we must work together and combine our human expertise with AI capabilities. This way, we can make sure healthcare delivery remains effective and patient-centred.

New Job Opportunities

Developing, implementing, and maintaining AI systems creates new job opportunities for data science, machine learning, and AI engineering graduates.

Healthcare providers will also need professionals who can interpret AI-generated insights, ensuring the technology aligns with ethical and medical standards.

Enhanced Efficiency and Productivity:

AI has the potential to streamline administrative tasks, allowing healthcare professionals to spend more of their time on patient care. This could result in better healthcare outcomes and increased demand for specific healthcare jobs.

Ethical and Regulatory Oversight:

As AI becomes more integrated into healthcare, professionals must oversee and regulate these technologies. Jobs related to ethics, policy development, and regulatory compliance may become more critical.

Bringing artificial intelligence (AI) into healthcare brings ethical and regulatory challenges. We must closely monitor how it's used to ensure it's responsible, safe, and fair for everyone involved. Some challenges we must consider include protecting patient autonomy, ensuring data privacy, ensuring algorithms are transparent, and ensuring fairness.

When using AI in healthcare, we must consider specific ethical considerations. For instance, AI systems often require access to sensitive personal health data, which raises concerns regarding data privacy and consent.

To maintain trust and uphold ethical standards, it's crucial to ensure that patient information remains confidential and that permission is obtained before using their AI systems data. At the same time, we must balance the benefits of AI-driven insights and patients' rights to control their personal information.

Another thing we need to remember regarding AI is the possibility of algorithm biases. It can lead to unequal outcomes and perpetuate healthcare disparities. AI systems must be trained on diverse, representative datasets to avoid this. Additionally, transparency in how AI algorithms make decisions is crucial to maintaining accountability, especially in high-stakes situations like diagnosis and treatment planning.

Our current legal frameworks need to be equipped to handle all its complexities. That's why regulatory bodies are working towards creating guidelines and standards that ensure AI tools' safety, effectiveness, and ethical use in healthcare settings. It includes setting clear criteria for testing and validating AI systems, monitoring real-world performance, and ensuring compliance with healthcare regulations.

We must address the challenges of sharing data across borders and the global development of AI in healthcare. We want to ensure everyone follows the same ethical and privacy standards. We must work together, including healthcare providers, AI developers, regulatory bodies, and patients, to create guidelines that ensure AI is used ethically and responsibly in healthcare.

Skill Development:

Healthcare professionals may need to adapt to the changes and acquire new skills. Continuous education and training programs can help individuals stay relevant and enhance their capabilities in the age of AI.

Policymakers, healthcare institutions, and educational systems must proactively address these concerns. Initiatives to reskill and upskill the workforce, as well as policies that ensure a fair transition, can help mitigate the negative impacts of AI on employment in the healthcare sector.

While job displacement is a valid concern, history has shown that technological advancements create new opportunities and often lead to previously unimaginable jobs. The responsible and thoughtful integration of AI in healthcare, combined with a focus on workforce development, can help balance technological progress and job stability.

In fear of risk, people losing their jobs over AI automation are the only healthcare providers who refuse to work alongside artificial intelligence.

Appendix A: Glossary of Key Terms

This glossary aims to provide a clear understanding of the key terms and concepts used in the field of AI in surgical robotics and automation. It is specifically tailored for non-technical readers interested in delving into this fascinating field.

Whether you're a healthcare professional, a patient, or simply someone curious about the advancements in surgical robotics, this glossary will help you navigate the terminology commonly used in this domain.

1. Artificial Intelligence (AI):

The simulation of human intelligence in machines programmed to learn, reason, and solve problems autonomously.

2. Robotics:

A branch of technology that designs, constructs, and operates robots capable of performing various tasks with precision and efficiency.

3. Surgical Robotics:

We use robotic systems to assist surgeons in performing complex surgical procedures with enhanced precision, control, and visualisation.

4. Automation:

They use technology and machines to perform tasks or processes without human intervention.

5. Machine Learning:

A subset of AI that enables machines to learn and improve from experience without explicit programming. It involves the development of algorithms that allow systems to automatically remember and make predictions or take actions based on data.

6. Computer-Assisted Surgery (CAS):

We are integrating computer technology into surgical procedures to aid and guide surgeons during preoperative planning, intraoperative navigation, and postoperative evaluation.

7. Haptic Feedback:

The tactile sensation or force feedback is provided to the surgeon through a robotic system, allowing them to perceive and manipulate objects in real time during surgery.

8. Telemedicine:

The remote provision of healthcare services using telecommunications technology enables medical professionals to diagnose, treat, and monitor patients from a distance.

9. Augmented Reality (AR):

The overlay of computer-generated visual information in the real-world environment provides surgeons with real-time guidance and additional information during procedures.

10. Internet of Medical Things (IoMT):

The network of interconnected medical devices, sensors, and software applications that collect and exchange data to improve patient care, enhance diagnosis, and optimise treatment.

11. Human-Machine Collaboration:

Integrating human expertise with machine capabilities allows surgeons and robotic systems to work together to achieve better surgical outcomes.

12. Ethical Considerations:

We are examining the moral, legal, and societal implications of AI in surgical robotics, including issues such as patient privacy, data security, and the responsibility of autonomous systems.

13. Autonomous Surgical Systems:

One of the most significant breakthroughs in surgical robotics is the development of autonomous surgical systems. These systems employ AI algorithms to perform complex surgical procedures with minimal human intervention.

14. Image Recognition and Augmented Reality:

This technology gives surgeons a more accurate understanding of a patient's anatomy and helps plan complex surgeries.

15. Predictive Analytics and Decision Support:

This capability empowers surgeons to make more informed decisions and personalise treatment plans based on individual patient characteristics, reducing risks and improving patient outcomes.

16. Robotic Assistance and Teleoperation:

AI-driven robotic assistants can collaborate with surgeons during minimally invasive procedures, enhancing precision and reducing the risk of human error. These robots can perform suturing, tissue manipulation, and instrument positioning under the surgeon's guidance. Additionally, teleoperation systems enable surgeons to remotely control robots, allowing them to perform surgeries from a distance, which is particularly beneficial in underserved areas or emergencies.

17. Surgical Training and Simulation:

AI-based surgical simulators provide a safe and immersive environment for surgeons to practice complex procedures before operating on patients. These simulators can replicate real-life scenarios, allowing surgeons to refine their skills, test new techniques, and gain experience without compromising patient safety.

DEFINITIONS

To introduce the readers to AI in Healthcare, the table below provides a list of definitions of the main terms and concepts used throughout this book.

Term used	Definition
AI	Artificial Intelligence
Algorithm	An algorithm is a step-by-step, well-defined set of instructions or a sequence of computational steps that, when followed, leads to accomplishing a specific task or solving a particular problem.
Data Analysis	Data analysis inspects, cleans, transforms, and models data to discover meaningful information, draw conclusions, and support decision-making.
Clinical Trial	A clinical trial is a systematic and scientific study conducted to assess the safety, efficacy, and potential side effects of a medical intervention,

	such as a new drug, medical device, treatment, or procedure, in human participants.
ML	Machine Learning: Machine Learning is a subfield of artificial intelligence (AI) that focuses on developing algorithms and models that enable computer systems to learn and improve their performance from experience and data without being explicitly programmed.
DL	Deep Learning: Deep learning is a type of machine learning where artificial **neural networks**, inspired by the human brain, learn to perform tasks directly from data.
Neural Networks	Neural networks are fundamental components in machine learning and deep learning, capable of capturing complex patterns and relationships within data.
CT	Computerised Tomography, commonly known as CT or CAT scan (Computed Axial Tomography), is a medical imaging technique that uses X-rays and computer processing to create detailed cross-sectional images of the body's internal structures.
Big Data	Big Data refers to large and diverse sets of information that are too complex to be processed by traditional methods.
NLP	Natural Language Processing is a branch of artificial intelligence focusing on the interaction between computers and human language.
GAN	Generative Adversarial Networks, or GANs, are a class of artificial intelligence algorithms used in unsupervised machine learning.
Computer Vision	Computer Vision is a field of artificial intelligence that empowers machines to interpret and understand visual information from the world,

	like how humans perceive and comprehend images or videos.
PCAs	A Picture Archiving and Communication System, commonly known as PACS, is a medical imaging technology that facilitates the acquisition, storage, retrieval, and distribution of digital medical images.
IoT	*Internet of Things*

Epilogue

As we close the final chapter of 'Artificial Intelligence in Healthcare,' we find ourselves standing at the threshold of a new healthcare frontier where innovation knows no bounds and the convergence of humanity and technology transforms the essence of healing.

The journey we embarked upon together has revealed the remarkable strides made in integrating artificial intelligence into the healthcare ecosystem. From the accelerated pace of diagnostics to the individualised precision of treatment plans, this book's pages have unfolded a profound change narrative. Yet, as we take a moment to reflect, it becomes evident that the story is far from over.

The epilogue of this exploration serves as both a reflection and a call to action. The integration of AI in healthcare is not a static phenomenon; it's a dynamic force, continually shaping and reshaping the landscape. The ethical considerations, the societal impacts, and the evolving role of healthcare professionals demand our constant attention and thoughtful engagement.

The stories shared within these pages are not just anecdotes of technological prowess but invitations to participate actively in the discourse surrounding the future of medicine. As we stand at this juncture, let us embrace our collective responsibility to ensure that the benefits of AI in healthcare are equitably distributed and that the ethical frameworks guiding its implementation remain steadfast.

Our epilogue is not an end but a prelude to the continued evolution of healthcare. In the future, collaboration between human empathy and artificial intelligence is not just a possibility but a necessity. As we move forward, may we be catalysts for change, advocates for ethical practices, and champions for a healthcare system that leverages technology to enhance the well-being of all?

In the spirit of discovery and progress, let 'Artificial Intelligence' be a catalyst for your exploration into the future of medicine—one that is inclusive, compassionate, and ever-adaptive to the changing tides of innovation. As we close this book, let us carry the lessons learned and the visions shared into the unfolding chapters of our own lives, contributing to a healthier, more connected, and technologically empowered world.

Afterword

Dear Reader,

As we stand on the other side of 'Artificial Intelligence in Healthcare,' the voyage we've shared unveils not just a glimpse but a profound immersion into the future of medicine. The concepts explored, the narratives unravelled, and the possibilities laid bare are not mere words on pages but stepping stones into uncharted territories.

This "afterword" is a moment of reflection, a pause in the journey, to consider the paths we've traversed and the roads yet to be discovered. The allure of artificial intelligence in healthcare is not confined to the tales we've told; it's an evolving narrative, beckoning us to contribute our chapters.
The narrative arc of this book touches on the transformative power of AI—from its potential to redefine diagnoses to its promise in tailoring treatments with unprecedented precision. Yet, it's essential to acknowledge that the story isn't complete. The ever-shifting landscapes of technology, ethics, and healthcare demand an ongoing dialogue and engagement.

In the chapters behind us, we've explored the ethical considerations accompanying AI integration, the societal impacts that ripple through communities, and the evolving roles of healthcare professionals. The afterword is an extension of this dialogue, an acknowledgement that our collective responsibility to shape the future of healthcare transcends the confines of this book.

It will inspire you to participate actively in the ongoing narrative as we move forward. The uncharted territories are not just realms of technological innovation; they are invitations to be advocates for responsible AI implementation.

The odyssey of tomorrow's healthcare is an adventure awaiting the daring. So, dear Reader, let this "afterword" guide you as you contribute your stories, insights, and perspectives to the unfolding tapestry of healthcare innovation.

With anticipation for the "chapters" you'll add to this grand narrative,

Constantine Leo Serafim MBSC

ABOUT THE BOOK

The narrative unfolds by representing a holistic view of how AI reshapes diagnosis, treatment, and patient care. Guided by the principle that knowledge empowers, our narrative weaves real-world examples, captivating stories, and expert insights to paint a vivid picture of how AI reshapes diagnostics, treatment strategies, and patient care.

What is Artificial Intelligence (AI)?
How is Artificial Intelligence used in healthcare?
How can AI Improve Healthcare?
What are the benefits of AI in Healthcare?
What does the Future Hold for AI in Healthcare?

"Artificial Intelligence in Healthcare" takes readers on a captivating journey into the future of medicine. It is where the synergy of artificial intelligence (AI) and healthcare promises transformative advancements.
You will read about AI's role in revolutionising Healthcare:

✓ AI in diagnosing diseases
✓ Potential benefits of AI in Medicine
✓ Understanding AI in Medicine
✓ Personalised medicine and treatments
✓ Misuse of Medical AI Tools and Risks
✓ New job opportunities and job transformation
✓ Ethical and regulatory oversight
✓ And a lot more...

The ebook is written in an accessible and non-technical style, delving into AI's profound impact on the healthcare landscape. This ebook is for non-technical enthusiasts as it simplifies the cutting-edge advancements revolutionising how we perceive, approach, and experience healthcare.

With an eye towards the future, the ebook speculates on upcoming innovations, encouraging readers to contemplate the evolving role of AI in their health journey. Whether you're a healthcare professional, a patient, or simply curious about the intersection of technology and well-being, " Artificial Intelligence in Healthcare" offers an engaging and informative glimpse into the promising landscape of AI-driven healthcare.

ABOUT THE AUTHOR

Constantine Leo Serafim is a true pioneer in computer science, boasting an impressive career that spanned over half a century. His unparalleled expertise and dedication left an indelible mark on the public and private sectors. His contributions to government and non-governmental organisation (NGO) projects were groundbreaking, shaping how we use technology to address societal challenges.

Throughout his illustrious career, Serafim's work was characterised by innovation and a tireless commitment to improving the world through technology. His involvement in government projects was instrumental in driving the digital transformation of public services. His leadership and visionary thinking paved the way for integrating cutting-edge technology into various government agencies, benefiting citizens and taxpayers alike.

Serafim has been an invaluable asset in NGOs, lending his technical expertise to various initiatives to address technical challenges. Whether it was developing innovative solutions to tackle complex challenges with people dealing with dementia, Serafim's influence was transformative.

His pioneering efforts led to the development of innovative solutions for people dealing with Alzheimer's that improved patient outcomes and revolutionised the way healthcare providers delivered services.

Beyond his work on NGO projects, Serafim was a prolific inventor known for his product designs and marketing strategies. His inventive spirit and keen business insight led to the creation of numerous products that not only met the needs of consumers but also pushed the boundaries of what was technologically possible. His ability to identify market trends and design products that resonated with consumers made him a force to be reckoned with in the business technical world.

Serafim's legacy extends far beyond his impressive resume and countless accomplishments. He mentored and inspired numerous aspiring computer scientists and innovators, nurturing the next generation of talent and ensuring his knowledge and passion for technology would continue to shape the future.

In summary, Serafim is a trailblazer in computer science, a visionary leader in NGO projects, a pioneer in healthcare services, and a prolific inventor and marketer. His contributions have left an enduring impact on the world, and his legacy inspires those who follow in his footsteps.

www.ingramcontent.com/pod-product-compliance
Lightning Source LLC
Chambersburg PA
CBHW070016300526
45794CB00001B/334